DIVERS
EQUITY,
INCLUSION
& TEACHING

DIVERSITY, EQUITY, INCLUSION & TEACHING

KULWINDER MAUDE
LUCY DAVIES

1 Oliver's Yard
55 City Road
London EC1Y 1SP

2455 Teller Road
Thousand Oaks
California 91320

Unit No 323-333, Third Floor, F-Block
International Trade Tower
Nehru Place, New Delhi – 110 019

8 Marina View Suite 43-053
Asia Square Tower 1
Singapore 018960

Editor: Amy Thornton
Senior project editor: Chris Marke
Cover design: Sheila Tong
Typeset by: C&M Digitals (P) Ltd, Chennai, India
Printed in the UK

© 2025 Lucy Davies and Kulwinder Maude. Also, Chapters 1, 3 and 4 Georgia Veness and Elizabeth Blakeman; Chapters 5 and 6 Amy Boyd; Chapter 7 Amy Boyd and Kieran Roper; Chapter 8 Rosie Legender.

First published in 2025

Apart from any fair dealing for the purposes of research or private study, or criticism or review, as permitted under the Copyright, Designs and Patents Act 1988, this publication may be reproduced, stored or transmitted in any form, or by any means, only with the prior permission in writing of the publishers, or in the case of reprographic reproduction, in accordance with the terms of licences issued by the Copyright Licensing Agency. Enquiries concerning reproduction outside those terms should be sent to the publishers.

Library of Congress Control Number: 2024951374

British Library Cataloguing in Publication Data

A catalogue record for this book is available from the British Library

ISBN 978-1-5296-8616-6
ISBN 978-1-5296-8615-9 (pbk)

CONTENTS

Acknowledgements	vi
About the authors and contributors	vii
Introduction	ix
1 Racism *Lucy Davies and Georgia Veness*	1
2 Economic injustice (class, social deprivation and poverty) *Lucy Davies*	18
3 Gender discrimination and sexism in schools *Georgia Veness*	35
4 Exclusion (disability) *Georgia Veness and Elizabeth Blakeman*	50
5 Challenging ableism and neuronormativity *Amy Boyd*	65
6 Communal identity *Amy Boyd*	83
7 Personal identity *Amy Boyd and Kieran Roper*	98
8 Globalisation and environmental deprivation *Rosie Legender, Lucy Davies and Kulwinder Maude*	119
Concluding remarks	140
References	145
Index	156

ACKNOWLEDGEMENTS

We would like to thank the students we have worked with at the School of Education at Durham University for embracing our sessions on Diversity, Equity and Inclusion and motivating us in looking for opportunities to embed such issues into our teaching. We would also like to thank Just Like Us who have helped us consider best practice for increasing LGBTQ+ visibility in ITT. Special thanks also go to Wingate Infants and Junior School who have given us first-hand experiences in poverty proofing the school day.

ABOUT THE AUTHORS AND CONTRIBUTORS

Kulwinder Maude is Assistant Professor (Teaching) at Durham University. She has over 26 years' experience working in different sectors of education, including extensive experience of teaching and learning in primary schools (England and India) as well as in UK higher education. She is the Programme Director for the BA (QTS) Three Year Programme for Initial Teacher Education and teaches undergraduate and postgraduate education courses. Her research interests include writing about English as an additional language (EAL), ethnicity, inclusion and issues related to teacher well-being and retention. She has also written articles and chapters on many aspects of primary English and EAL for initial teacher education (ITE) and primary school practitioners.

Lucy M. Davies is Assistant Professor in Humanities in Primary Education in the School of Education at Durham University, having been a primary school teacher in the North East of England. She is the Programme Director for the PGCE Primary course and teaches undergraduate and postgraduate education courses. Her research interests are in diversity, equity and inclusion in the classroom and student engagement in learning, as well as creative thinking.

Georgia Veness is a full-time Year 4 classroom teacher at an independent school in Brighton. Most recently she has taken up a new position in an international school in Thailand. She studied for her Primary Education degree at Durham University and graduated with a first, specialising in EAL. She is very keen to develop her classroom practice and expertise in EAL, as well as supporting classroom teachers in establishing links between classroom practice and research for EAL pupils.

Amy Boyd studied for her Primary Education degree at Durham University and graduated with a first-class dissertation, focusing on free school meal children's reading attainment in the year 2023–4. She is furthering her studies with a Master's Degree at Durham University, specialising in Educational Leadership and Change, enriching her teaching understanding and pedagogy before undertaking a full-time primary teacher role. She is very keen to develop her classroom practice and expertise in creating an inclusive classroom encouraging diversity and equity, as well as supporting classroom teachers in establishing links between classroom practice and research for all pupils.

Rosie Legender studied for her Primary Education degree at Durham University. She graduated with a first-class dissertation, focusing on the teaching of 'critical cultural awareness' in geography education and its importance in rejecting the stereotypes of distant places. After graduating from Durham, Rosie became a primary school teacher in London. She has now successfully completed her first early career teacher (ECT) year where she has created an inclusive, safe and happy learning environment for her students; Rosie is looking forward to continuing her primary education career this year.

Elizabeth Blakeman is in the final year of her degree studying Primary Education at Durham University. Alongside her studies, she has developed a strong passion for deaf education and is advancing her British Sign Language (BSL) skills as she works towards specialising in teaching deaf children. Elizabeth is committed to creating an inclusive classroom where every child, regardless of hearing ability, can thrive. Upon finishing her degree, she plans to immerse herself in hands-on teaching, applying her skills to create dynamic and supportive learning environments that bridge the gap between theory and practice.

Kieran Roper qualified as a primary school teacher from Durham University in 2024. During his time at Durham, he advocated for EDI issues and researched on topics such as raising LGBTQ+ visibility in the primary curriculum. Kieran is committed to creating an inclusive classroom environment through diverse resources and curriculum choices.

INTRODUCTION

KULWINDER MAUDE

In the current globalised and increasingly interconnected world, primary school teachers play a crucial role in shaping the minds and values of young children. Understanding and implementing diversity, equity and inclusion (DEI) in teaching is essential for fostering a learning environment that is both fair and conducive to the holistic development of all children who are the citizens of tomorrow.

Here, we would like to take the opportunity to tell our readers more about the *foundational principles* of DEI that have guided our work throughout this book in our attempt to create a fair, respectful and supportive environment in primary classrooms.

DIVERSITY

- *Recognition of differences*: Acknowledging and valuing the various dimensions of diversity, including but not limited to race, ethnicity, gender, sexual orientation, socio-economic status, ability, religion and cultural background.

- *Representation*: Striving for representation of diverse groups in all areas, including leadership positions, curricula and media, to ensure that all voices and perspectives are included and valued right from the start in primary education.

- *Cultural competence*: Developing the ability to understand, communicate with and effectively interact with people across different cultures and backgrounds. This includes continuous learning and adaptation to diverse cultural contexts in the school environment.

EQUITY

- *Fairness and justice*: Ensuring that policies, practices and resources are designed and implemented to address disparities and provide all children with the support they need to succeed in school.

- *Access to opportunities*: Guaranteeing equal access to educational, professional and social opportunities for all, particularly those from historically marginalised or underserved groups.

- *Individualised support*: Recognising and addressing the unique needs and circumstances of each individual child to remove barriers and enable their full participation and achievement.

INCLUSION

- *Belonging and respect*: Creating environments where all children feel respected, accepted and valued. This involves fostering a sense of belonging and ensuring that everyone can participate fully and authentically.

- *Engagement and participation*: Actively involving diverse pupils and groups in decision-making processes and activities, ensuring their input and perspectives shape outcomes and policies related to teaching and learning within the classroom and wider school network.

- *Safe and supportive environments*: Establishing spaces where children feel safe from discrimination, harassment and exclusion, and where their well-being and dignity are prioritised.

INTERRELATED PRINCIPLES

- *Intersectionality*: Recognising and addressing the interconnected nature of social categorisations such as race, gender and class, which can create overlapping and interdependent systems of discrimination or disadvantage.

- *Continuous improvement*: Committing to ongoing evaluation and improvement of policies, practices and attitudes related to DEI in schools. This involves regular assessment, feedback and adaptation to ensure effectiveness and responsiveness to changing needs and contexts within the educational environment.

- *Accountability and transparency*: Ensuring that schools and pupils are accountable for their actions and decisions regarding DEI. This includes being transparent about goals, progress and challenges, and being open to scrutiny and feedback.

APPLICATION IN EDUCATION

Based on the principles of DEI, in this book we have signposted various strategies and ideas that can be implemented to develop an *inclusive curriculum*. We believe that by developing and delivering curricula that reflect diverse perspectives and experiences, we can ensure that all children see themselves represented and respected in their education. Through relevant case studies and reflective questioning, we encourage *equitable assessment* in classrooms. Implementing fair assessment methods that recognise and accommodate the diverse needs and strengths of all pupils and avoiding biases that may disadvantage any group are essential to creating a sense of fairness in the school experience. This book will also support *teaching practices* by signposting teaching methods that are inclusive and supportive of diverse learning styles and needs, fostering an environment where every child can thrive.

SOCIETAL IMPACT

Through this book we advocate humbly for social justice, promoting broader societal change which would advocate for policies and practices that support equity, diversity and inclusion beyond the immediate environment of primary schools.

We encourage community engagement through building strong, respectful relationships with diverse communities within the school vicinity and beyond (if applicable), understanding their needs and perspectives, and working collaboratively to address common goals and challenges. Finally, we hope to contribute to global awareness by encouraging a global perspective on diversity and inclusion, recognising the interconnectedness of people and issues worldwide, and promoting solidarity and understanding across borders.

By adhering to these principles, teachers and school leaders can create environments that not only respect and celebrate diversity, but also actively work to dismantle barriers to equity and inclusion, fostering a more just and inclusive school environment and society for all by extension.

This book has been written in collaboration with university-based teacher educators, ECTs and undergraduate trainee teachers. When we thought of writing a book on the role of DEI in teaching, we had to articulate for ourselves in depth reasons for collaborating on such a project. Our team is made up of our former and current trainee teachers who aim to and are teaching with the above-mentioned DEI principles in mind. At all times, as a team, we have attempted to:

PROMOTE FAIRNESS AND EQUAL OPPORTUNITIES

Equity in education should ensure that all children, regardless of their background or personal circumstances, have access to the same educational opportunities. We believe that primary school teachers need to recognise and address the diverse needs of their pupils to provide an equitable learning experience. This might involve differentiating learning objectives, providing additional support for children who need it and removing barriers that may hinder the learning process. By promoting fairness, teachers can help bridge the achievement gap and ensure that every pupil has the chance to succeed.

REFLECT SOCIETAL DIVERSITY

Classrooms today are microcosms of the broader society, often comprising children from various cultural, ethnic and socio-economic backgrounds. Primary school teachers must understand and respect this diversity, creating an inclusive environment where all pupils feel valued and respected. Recognising and celebrating diversity helps children develop a sense of belonging and self-worth, which is critical for their social and emotional development. It also prepares them to thrive in a multicultural society by fostering respect and appreciation for different perspectives and experiences.

ENCOURAGE CRITICAL THINKING AND EMPATHY

We know that incorporating DEI principles into the curriculum will help children develop critical thinking and empathy. When teachers expose pupils to diverse perspectives and encourage discussions about equity and inclusion, they help them understand and challenge biases and stereotypes. This promotes a more comprehensive worldview and encourages children to think critically about social issues. Furthermore, fostering empathy through understanding diverse experiences helps build a more compassionate and socially responsible generation; primary teachers have a key role to play in it.

PREPARE CHILDREN FOR A GLOBALISED WORLD

In an increasingly globalised world, the ability to navigate and appreciate diversity is a valuable skill. Primary school teachers who prioritise DEI prepare their pupils for future interactions in diverse workplaces and communities. By teaching children to value and engage with different cultures and viewpoints from an early age, teachers help them develop the intercultural competence needed to succeed in a globalised society. This competence includes communication skills, adaptability and the ability to work collaboratively with people from various backgrounds.

ADDRESS SYSTEMIC INEQUITIES

Education is a powerful tool for addressing systemic inequities and promoting social justice. Primary school teachers, by understanding and implementing EDI principles, can contribute to the dismantling of prejudiced systems and practices within education. This involves recognising and challenging discriminatory practices, advocating for policies that promote inclusion and being mindful of the diverse needs of their pupils. By doing so, teachers can help create a more just and equitable education system that benefits all children.

ENHANCE ACADEMIC AND SOCIAL OUTCOMES

Research has shown that inclusive educational practices can lead to improved academic and social outcomes for all children. When teachers create a supportive and inclusive classroom environment, pupils are more likely to engage in learning and exhibit positive behaviours. This is because an inclusive environment reduces feelings of alienation and increases children's motivation and self-esteem. Furthermore, diversity in the classroom enriches the learning experience by exposing pupils to different ideas and perspectives, fostering creativity and innovation.

IN THIS BOOK

In this book you will find ideas, strategies and resources to support primary school teachers in understanding the role of DEI in education in order to create a fair, respectful, and enriching learning environment. We truly believe that by embracing DEI principles teachers can promote fairness, reflect societal diversity, encourage critical thinking and empathy, prepare children for a globalised world, address systemic inequities and enhance academic and social outcomes. This understanding is crucial for nurturing well-rounded individuals who can contribute positively to a diverse and inclusive society.

Chapter 1 on *Racism* supports teachers in understanding and addressing racism in primary schools which is crucial for creating a safe, inclusive and supportive learning environment. It focuses on familiarising teachers with key aspects of racism in primary schools that they should know about, along with strategies to tackle it effectively. Readers will learn about forms of racism which can manifest in overt actions, such as racial slurs or exclusion, and subtle behaviours, like microaggressions or biased assumptions. Teachers must recognise both explicit and implicit forms of racism to address them effectively. We know that unchecked racism or racist behaviours can negatively impact children; experiencing or witnessing racism can leave indelible marks on children, which can manifest itself as lower self-esteem, academic challenges and emotional distress. Teachers should understand the serious implications of racism on students' well-being and academic performance.

Chapter 2 focuses on understanding the impact of *economic injustice* (which refers to the unequal distribution of wealth, resources and opportunities in society) on academic attainment. Readers learn about how it leads to disparities in income, education and quality of life, manifesting in various forms, such as poverty, lack of access to quality education and inadequate healthcare. Through case studies and reflective strategies, we look at how economic injustice can severely affect children's academic performance, mental and physical health, and overall well-being. Pupils from low-income families face challenges such as inadequate nutrition, lack of school supplies, limited access to extracurricular activities and less parental involvement due to economic constraints most of the time. As a teacher you will learn how economic injustice is often perpetuated by systemic factors such as discriminatory policies, lack of investment in marginalised communities and economic policies that favour the wealthy. Teachers should recognise that these systemic issues require broad-based solutions beyond the classroom.

Chapter 3 focuses on understanding *gender discrimination and sexism* in schools (referring to unfair treatment based on an individual's gender), which can result in unequal access to resources, opportunities and treatment. This chapter supports understanding of how sexism manifests as attitudes, behaviours, or institutional practices that devalue or marginalise individuals based on their gender. You will learn more about how gender discrimination and sexism can impact academic performance, confidence and participation in school life. Persistent sexism can also lead to decreased self-esteem, anxiety and depression among affected pupils. Social dynamics can be affected when sexism influences social interactions, fostering environments where gender stereotypes are reinforced, and bullying or harassment may occur. Teachers develop strategies to challenge biases and bring about systemic change in the school culture.

Chapter 4 encourages teachers to explore how notions of *exclusion through disability* impact children in schools. The chapter introduces practices and attitudes that prevent children with disabilities from fully participating in educational and social activities. This can include physical barriers, lack of appropriate resources and social stigmatisation. It is important to understand the challenges faced by children with disabilities in accessing the curriculum, leading to lower academic performance if accommodations are not provided. Exclusion can lead to social isolation, bullying and a lack of peer support, which can affect the emotional well-being of pupils with disabilities. Strategies that can be implemented to create an inclusive classroom environment through technology, peer support, developing anti-bullying policies and working closely with families and communities are outlined.

Chapter 5 supports teachers to develop understanding and learn how to challenge *ableism and neuronormativity* in the primary classroom. Following a review of the SEND improvement plan, due to be released in 2025, it is imperative for teachers to understand how attitudes linked with discrimination and social prejudice against people with disabilities, rooted in the belief that typical abilities are superior (ableism), can affect children with disability. The chapter enhances understanding about neuronormativity, which is the assumption that there is a standard or 'normal' way of brain functioning and behaviour, often marginalising those with neurological differences such as autism, ADHD, dyslexia and other neurodiverse conditions. This can give rise to stereotypes and misconceptions because of assumptions that students with disabilities or neurodiverse conditions are less capable. If they go unchecked, use of derogatory language or negative attitudes towards children with disabilities or neurodiverse conditions can create an atmosphere of undesirable language in the classroom. Furthermore, systemic barriers like lack of accommodations, rigid teaching methods and inflexible policies may result from not considering diverse learning needs. The chapter provides strategies to reduce impact on children in terms of academic achievement, mental health and wider social integration.

Chapter 6 focuses on building understanding about *communal identity*, which refers to the sense of belonging and shared identity that children feel with their school community and family background. This can be based on various factors such as ethnicity, culture, religion, language, or shared experiences and values. We emphasise that communal identity helps pupils develop a sense of belonging, self-esteem and social cohesion. It plays a crucial role in the overall development and well-being of children. When communal identity is facilitated in the primary classroom, teachers feel comfortable teaching about traditions, customs, languages and celebrations that are unique to a particular community linked with the school. Highlighting the role of shared values and beliefs of a school community or family background, etc. helps in creating collective memory which supports resilience and a sense of security.

Chapter 7 builds from communal identity (Chapter 6) to issues related to *personal identity*. Teachers engage in depth with an individual's sense of self, encompassing various aspects such as race, ethnicity, gender, sexual orientation, religion, socio-economic status, abilities, interests and values. The chapter enhances understanding of the fact that personal identity evolves over time through experiences, relationships and self-reflection. It also plays a crucial role in children's overall development and well-being which results in stronger self-esteem and confidence, positive mental health and confident social relationships. This chapter focuses particularly on marginalised communities of LGBTQ+ pupils in schools. Teachers are introduced to challenges faced by LGBTQ+ communities historically and what can be done to mitigate feelings of marginalisation and promote tolerance.

Chapter 8 introduces teachers to *global challenges and environmental deprivation* that children in our schools are exposed to in our modern globalised world. By global challenges we mean large-scale issues that affect people worldwide and require collective action to address. These include climate change, poverty, inequality and health crises, for example. Environmental deprivation refers to the lack of access to clean air, water, green spaces and safe living conditions. It often affects marginalised communities disproportionately, which we are keen to highlight to teachers. Both global challenges and environmental deprivation impact children negatively by affecting their health, academic performance and overall quality of life. Poor environmental conditions can lead to higher rates of illness, lower academic achievement and reduced opportunities. This chapter equips teachers with the understanding and strategies to mitigate the negative impact of both global challenges and environmental deprivation in the primary classroom.

KEY DEFINITIONS

Here are some terms which you will encounter throughout this book:

Identity: Identity is the unique set of characteristics which can be used to identify a person as themselves. It encompasses the values people hold, which help dictate the choices they make.

Discrimination: Discrimination is the unfair or prejudicial treatment of people or groups of people based on their characteristics such as race, ethnicity, religion, gender, age or sexual orientation.

Inclusion: Inclusion is the state or action of including or of being included within a group or structure. It is the practice of providing equal access to opportunities and resources for people who might otherwise be excluded.

Equality: Equality is the state of being equal, especially regarding the rights, status and opportunities that an individual has.

Marginalised: This is when an individual, group or concept is marginalised as insignificant or peripheral. It is the act of isolating and/or disempowering a person or group.

We hope you enjoy reading and learning more about the value of diversity, equity and inclusion in teaching as much as we have enjoyed writing this book for you.

1
RACISM
LUCY DAVIES AND GEORGIA VENESS

> **THIS CHAPTER**
>
> The chapter will provide opportunities for readers to reflect upon:
>
> - practices within schools that assist children with different cultural backgrounds
> - potential negative attitudes towards multiculturalism still existing in society today
> - events outside school that may affect children from different cultural backgrounds in the school community
> - conscious and/unconscious racial stereotypes and biases that may still influence teachers and learners' primary school experiences.

DEFINITIONS

To begin this chapter, we highlight some of the key terms and definitions that you may come across.

- *Race*: a word first used in the 16th century as European countries such as Britain, Spain, Portugal and France began to colonise parts of the world and started engaging with *eugenics*, which is the practice or advocacy of improving the human species by selectively mating people with specific desirable hereditary traits. 'Race' remains a word to describe groups that humans are often divided into based on physical traits regarded as common among people of shared ancestry. There is an increasing recognition that race is more of a social construct than a biological categorisation.

- *Ethnicity*: may be construed as an inherited or societally imposed construct. Ethnicities tend to be defined by a shared cultural heritage, ancestry, history, homeland, language, dialects, religion, or physical appearance (among other factors). Ethnicity is somewhat more nuanced than race and those of the same race may include various ethnicities.

- *Non-racist*: a non-racist person is not racist themselves, but they will be silent or be bystanders in the face of racism even when it makes them feel uncomfortable.

- *Anti-racist*: a person who is not racist and looks for opportunities to show that racism is not acceptable, proactively addressing racist attitudes and/or behaviours.

- *A note on the term BAME*: following the *Inclusive Britain* report (gov.uk, 2022) issued in March 2022, the UK government no longer uses the term 'BAME' which has been historically and frequently used to group all ethnic minorities together. This can disguise huge differences in outcomes between ethnic groups, further complicating the picture of educational attainment across different ethnic groups (RDU, 2022).

INTRODUCTION

The newly published Anti-Racism Initial Teacher Training (ITT) Framework (Lander and Smith, 2024) establishes that racism exists within society. Understanding racism is a learning journey for both adults and children alike. We are not expected to know all of the answers. Reflection and eagerness to learn are key to examining preconceptions. It is important to speak openly and positively about race, have regular discussions about it and to acknowledge how both race and racism impact people differently at various stages of their life. This chapter establishes that, despite some societal progress, barriers to learning about the racial injustices still exist in educational environments. The chapter also examines the concepts of race, ethnicity and their relationship to attainment levels and cultural engagement within schools and seeks to support readers by providing examples of inclusive resources – for example, multicultural children's literature and engaging with active listening activities.

RACE VS ETHNICITY

Race and *ethnicity* are distinct concepts that, while often used interchangeably, have different meanings and implications. Race, on the one hand, is primarily associated with physical characteristics such as somebody's skin colour, facial structure and features, and hair texture, and is often used to categorise individuals based on perceived biological differences. Ethnicity, on the other hand, relates to cultural factors such as nationality, language, religion and customs. It is more about shared cultural identity and heritage. For example, someone might identify racially as black but ethnically as Jamaican. The distinction is important because race is typically linked to historical and social dynamics and influences a person's socio-economic status and opportunities, as we will discuss later in this chapter, whereas ethnicity emphasises cultural connections (such as a shared *lingua franca*) and shared customs of a particular geographical area. Understanding these differences helps us to appreciate the complexity of identity and the different experiences faced by individuals from different backgrounds and heritages.

POLICIES AND LEGISLATION

Policies and legislation in the UK aim to combat racism in schools and ensure equal opportunities for all children. The Equality Act 2010 (DfE, 2010) is the foundation of this framework, prohibiting discrimination on the grounds of race, among other protected characteristics, in schools and all facets of life in Britain. This Act requires schools to promote equality and encourage good relations between different racial groups. Additionally, the Public Sector Equality Duty, also part of the Equality Act, requires schools to actively work to eliminate discrimination, advance equality of opportunity and foster good relations among its students. The DfE's guidance on preventing and tackling bullying (DfE, 2012) also addresses racist bullying, urging schools to implement robust anti-bullying policies so that all children can learn with the safety of not being bullied due to their race. Ofsted also evaluates how well schools promote equality and tackle discrimination during inspections. Together, these policies and legislative measures create a framework that encourages schools to create inclusive environments and ensure all children have equal opportunities to succeed.

THE PICTURE IN THE UK

Racism remains an issue in the UK due to deep-rooted systemic and structural inequalities that perpetuate discriminatory attitudes and practices. Historical ties to colonialism and the British Empire (which once had control over British India, for example) have created racial hierarchies and biases that are ingrained in the wider British society. These biases, unfortunately, continue to influence contemporary social, economic and political institutions. Despite legal frameworks (like the Equality Act 2010) that aim to combat discrimination, these measures alone are insufficient to break the deep-rooted prejudices that sadly exist across all parts of the UK. Racial stereotypes and implicit biases persist, often influencing behaviours and decisions unconsciously, thereby reinforcing cycles of inequality. Furthermore, socio-economic disparities among ethnic minorities, driven by factors such as access to equal and high-quality education, employment opportunities and healthcare, exacerbate the challenges they face. The lack of diverse representation in leadership positions and media further hinders efforts to address and rectify these issues, as perspectives in organisations are limited and fewer solutions are considered in both policy-making and public discussions.

Various recent events have also contributed to the persistence of racist attitudes in the UK. The 2016 Brexit referendum and its aftermath have heightened nationalist sentiments and xenophobia (a dislike of, or prejudice against people from other countries), leading to an increase in hate crimes and discrimination against immigrants and ethnic minorities. The global Black Lives Matter movement, ignited by the murder of George Floyd in the United States in May 2020, has also shed light on racial injustices in the UK, prompting widespread protests and calls for action against systemic racism, particularly within the police force and employment institutions. For example, according to a report released by End Violence Against Women (Geoghegan, 2022), 10 per cent of women are less likely to report sexual assault to the police following the Sarah Everard case. Black people are 9.7 times more likely than white people to be stopped and searched by police and are 40 times more likely to be stopped and searched under the controversial Section 60 power, which has risen as the government has tried to crack down on knife crime (Shutti et al., 2020). No police officers were prosecuted over the death of Jean Charles De Menezez, who was shot by police in 2005, and, in a following investigation in 2016, the European Court of Human Rights did not find the police force guilty either. More recently, the COVID-19 pandemic has disproportionately impacted ethnic minority communities, exposing deep-rooted health and economic inequalities, due to the trend of lower wages and limited access to healthcare that these minority groups receive. Reports of racially motivated attacks against East Asian communities surged, fuelled by misinformation and xenophobic scapegoating related to the origin of the virus. These events have highlighted the urgent call-to-arms to address racism and take steps to ensure equality and justice for all individuals in the UK, regardless of what their ethnic background may be.

Philips (2005) suggested that the 'UK is sleepwalking into segregation' because communities stay separate and don't participate in shared activities together. Communities in the UK continue to be segregated due to the interplay of historical, socio-economic and cultural factors. Decades of immigration and colonialism have contributed to the formation of segregated ethnic communities, where individuals and families from similar backgrounds cluster together – for example, in places like Blackburn and Lancashire which are home to diverse numbers of South Asian immigrants. Socio-economic disparities further perpetuate segregation, as lower-income groups often have limited housing options and may be concentrated in specific areas, leading to pockets of poverty and isolation throughout the UK. Cultural differences and language barriers also play a role, with immigrants and minority groups often gravitating towards neighbourhoods where they feel a sense of belonging and familiarity.

Hate crimes have also become more prevalent in recent years due to a variety of factors. In 2023 alone, hate crimes relating to race accounted for a majority of police recorded hate crimes (70 per cent; 101,906 offences), affecting not just the victims involved, but also their wider communities. Table 1.1 displays hate crime prevalence from 2019–2023 according to different demographics, with racially motivated hate crimes being by far the most prevalent. It should be noted here that more people are reporting these crimes or feel that they can – which does reflect how we are talking more and more about race, therefore removing any stigma in wider societies.

Table 1.1   Hate crime prevalence between 2019 and 2023 (www.gov.uk/government/collections/hate-crime-statistics)

Hate crime strand	2018/19	2019/20	2020/21	2021/22	2022/23	% change 2021/22 to 2022/23
Race	77,850	[x]	90,909	108,476	101,906	-6
Religion	8,460	[x]	6,288	8,602	8,241	-4
Sexual orientation	14,161	[x]	18,239	25,639	24,102	-6
Disability	8,052	[x]	9,690	13,905	13,777	-1
Transgender	2,253	[x]	2,728	4,262	4,732	11
Total number of offences	104,765	112,633	122,256	153,536	145,214	-5

Other events outside the classroom/education may affect children from different cultural backgrounds in the school community. For instance, a sharp increase in hate crimes occurred after the Manchester bombings of 2017, with school-aged children being the victims of some of these offences.

THE INTERSECTION BETWEEN RACE AND POVERTY

In the UK, the intersection between race and poverty is a complex issue shaped by historical, social and economic factors. Ethnic minorities are disproportionately affected by poverty, often due to structured barriers in education, employment and housing. Structural racism is displayed through lower wages, higher unemployment rates and limited access to social mobility for people from ethnic minority backgrounds. These challenges are compounded by discriminatory practices and biases within institutions, leading to the continuation of socio-economic disparities. This therefore means that the effects of poverty are more severe for ethnic minority communities, influencing the health of individuals, educational attainment and overall quality of life.

Pakistani and Bangladeshi people were the most likely of all ethnic groups to live in the most deprived neighbourhoods (where each neighbourhood typically contains about 1,500 residents) in England according to the Index of Multiple Deprivation (https://data.cdrc.ac.uk/dataset/index-multiple-deprivation-imd). This reflects that higher proportions of their fellow residents (of any ethnicity) experience a range of deprivations and are most heavily influenced by deprivation relating to low income or being involuntarily excluded from the labour market. Approximately three out of ten Pakistani and Bangladeshi people live in the most income-deprived 10 per cent of neighbourhoods (Khan, 2020). Addressing these disparities would require country-wide targeted policies that tackled both racial inequality and economic disadvantage, ensuring equitable opportunities and support for all communities.

RACISM IN UK SCHOOLS

Racism is a significant problem in UK schools which adversely affects the educational outcomes of children from ethnic minority backgrounds. This racism can manifest in various ways, such as racial bullying, stereotyping by teachers and lower academic expectations. These discriminatory practices create a hostile learning environment, leading to increased stress, reduced self-esteem and sometimes the self-fulfilling prophecy among affected students. The self-fulfilling prophecy is a psychological concept where an individual's expectations or beliefs about a situation or themselves can cause those expectations to come true. For instance, if an ethnic minority student believes that they are less capable, then, due to racial stereotypes, their teacher views them as less capable and therefore focuses their attention elsewhere, which can then lead to the student performing poorly. This poor performance then reinforces the student's original belief that they are less capable, creating a vicious cycle.

As a result of this discrimination, children from ethnic minority backgrounds may disengage from studies, participate less in class and have higher absenteeism rates. Moreover, the lack of representation in the curriculum and racial stereotypes held by teaching staff can make these students feel alienated and undervalued. These factors contribute to a wider achievement gap, with ethnic minority students often performing below their potential.

> If the evidence that we can get points to there being an epidemic of racism in schools and yet there is no reliable data at a national level, then the government can't guarantee that they're meeting basic safeguarding let alone producing a world-class education system. It suggests that the government's attitude is, at best, one of ignorance and disinterest.
>
> (Gillborn, 2024)

TEACHER RACIAL BIAS

Research from Mirza (1992) found that racist teachers were one of the main causes of racism in schools. These teachers fell into three categories: first, being *colour blind* – teachers who believed that all pupils were equal but did not challenge racism they witnessed in school. *Liberal chauvinists* were teachers who believed that black pupils were culturally deprived and therefore had lower expectations of them. *Overt racists* were teachers who believed that black pupils were inferior and actively discriminated against them. Although this research is dated, it clearly demonstrates how racist teachers impacted the educational outcomes of their pupils a relatively short time ago. Gillborn's (2005) research sheds light on the pervasive issue of racial bias in schools. This study found that teachers often labelled black students as disruptive or problematic at a disproportionate rate compared to their peers of other races. This bias can have profound consequences for black students, affecting their academic performance, self-esteem and overall well-being. Addressing these biases and promoting equity in education is crucial for creating a more inclusive and just learning environment for all students.

Unconscious racial bias among teachers can profoundly impact the educational experiences of ethnic minority students. Teachers may unknowingly hold stereotypes and prejudices that influence their perceptions and interactions with these students. This bias can manifest in various ways, such as lower expectations of academic achievement for ethnic minority groups, harsher discipline for these children, or subtle forms of favouritism towards students who align more closely with dominant cultural norms. These biases not only hinder the academic and social development of ethnic minority students, but also perpetuate inequalities within schools.

Racially motivated peer-on-peer bullying also contributes to the racism still experienced in UK schools. This form of bullying involves targeting individuals based on their race or ethnicity, perpetuating harmful stereotypes and creating a climate of exclusion and discrimination. Victims of racially motivated bullying often experience distress, anxiety and a sense of isolation, which can have long-lasting effects on their academic attainment and mental health. In addition to this, witnessing or experiencing racism in school can create a hostile learning environment, hindering the educational experience for all students. To address this issue, schools must take proactive measures to prevent and address racially motivated bullying, including implementing anti-bullying policies, providing education on diversity and inclusion, and encouraging a culture of respect among students. It is essential for educators and administrators to create safe spaces where students feel empowered to speak out against racism and where all individuals are valued and respected, regardless of their race or ethnicity.

Meanwhile, there is evidence to suggest more needs to be done to address trainee teachers' attitudes to racism and ethnicity (Shah and Coles, 2020). When teachers are trained to consider ethnicity and the impact of racism, anti-racist teaching is more practicable. Currently, it seems that trainee teachers hold more negative views of ethnic minority students in diverse schools than in less diverse schools compared to qualified teachers, suggesting it is crucial for teachers to experience ethnic minority students to tackle negative preconceived ideas.

A positive step in recent years, many schools have made efforts to *decolonise* the curriculum in an attempt to make it non-racist and one that actively promotes DEI representation of all racial and ethnic groups. Creating a non-racist curriculum, however, can create several challenges for teachers and policy-makers. One significant issue is the lack of diversity among teaching staff and curriculum developers, which can result in blind spots and biases in the resources and perspectives being presented to students. Additionally, there may be resistance from stakeholders who are reluctant to acknowledge or confront the systemic inequalities embedded within existing educational structures. Currently, many young people do not feel supported by their teachers when it comes to exclusion and/or bullying based on their race. Recent research by Sapouna et al. (2023) found widespread examples of young people and parents reporting that they felt teachers were dismissive of racial bias or stereotyping.

Addressing these issues requires comprehensive reforms to current curriculum plans that go beyond simply diversifying reading lists or adding tokenistic content to pre-existing curriculum plans. In order to be successful in creating a non-racist curriculum, educators must re-evaluate their school's entire approach to education to ensure that all aspects, from curriculum design to assessment methods, actively promote anti-racism and foster inclusivity. This creates an immense workload for educators who may not have the time to completely overhaul their whole school's approach to teaching. Furthermore, educators may move on to different schools, leaving the work to new teachers who may have different ideas on how to create a non-racist learning environment, posing the question of who the responsibility lies with. Is it enough to expect schools to complete this overhaul within their own institutions, or should the government take more steps to help promote equality and diversity in all UK schools?

REFLECTION 1.1

Think about what teachers can do in the classroom to encourage better understanding of diverse cultures and promote tolerance in society.

What are some steps you could take in your own practice?

What practical steps could your school take to tackle some of the issues highlighted?

How could racist bullying be addressed?

How could staff meetings and continuous professional development (CPD) be used to develop an inclusive curriculum?

ETHNIC MINORITY REPRESENTATION IN SCHOOLS

Racism and a lack of representation of ethnic minority children in schools might cause those children to feel invisible in school. The lack of representation in the school curriculum, textbooks and teaching staff that reflect the cultural backgrounds of ethnic minority children cause them to feel marginalised and disconnected from their peers and the learning environment. Additionally, subtle forms of bias and discrimination, whether intentional or unintentional, can contribute to feelings of invisibility among these students. Limited opportunities for cultural expression or celebration within the school community can also reinforce a sense of alienation and the lack of diversity among teaching staff can result in the lack of cultural celebration due to unawareness of other cultural customs, celebrations and practices. Furthermore, socio-economic disparities may intersect with ethnicity, leading to unequal access to resources and extra-curricular opportunities outside school due to poverty and placing different values on education, exacerbating feelings of invisibility and isolation. In such an environment, ethnic minority children may struggle to see themselves reflected positively and may feel overlooked or undervalued, impacting their sense of belonging and academic achievement.

UNINTENTIONAL RACISM IN SCHOOLS

Ethnocentrism refers to the view that one (often the dominant) culture has priority over others, often leading to biased perceptions and judgements about other cultures that are based on preconceived ideas. It is one of the main causes of unintentional racism in schools and can manifest in various ways, from curriculum choices that prioritise the perspectives and achievements of the dominant cultural group to unknown racial prejudices held by teachers which can lead to racist interactions between teachers and students, where students from minority backgrounds may feel marginalised or invisible.

CURRICULUM BIAS

Curriculum bias within UK schools refers to the tendency for educational resources, content and teaching methods to prioritise the perspectives, experiences and achievements of individuals from Britain and characters from its own history (mainly white, European, Christian people), marginalising and failing to represent or consider those from ethnic minority groups. This bias creates a narrow and incomplete understanding of history, literature and other subjects, which can lead to disengagement from ethnic minority students. By centring the curriculum around the history of Britain and the British perspective, the curriculum reinforces pre-existing ideas about race and exacerbates inequalities, further isolating ethnic minority students. Many schools have tried to combat this without overhauling the entire curriculum by introducing ideas such as 'cultural calendars' – aimed at celebrating a more diverse array of cultures and their celebrations. Schools also incorporate token 'special' days which celebrate diversity and cultural differences. The risks involved with adding these tokenistic days to the school calendar are vast, as they clearly highlight the ethnocentrism embedded in the national curriculum, where the content covered in these 'special' days is not apparent; these 'add-on' days thus present as merely afterthoughts.

In school, role models from ethnic minority backgrounds play a vital role in inspiring and empowering students from diverse backgrounds. Representation matters, especially in schools, where students often look to teachers, mentors and leaders for guidance and inspiration. Diverse role models serve as inspiring examples of what is possible, breaking down stereotypes and demonstrating the value of diversity in education. By sharing their experiences, knowledge and expertise, role models from ethnic minority backgrounds help to encourage and motivate students facing similar challenges and barriers and cultivate a more inclusive environment where all students can see themselves reflected and can feel inspired to reach their full potential.

ETHNIC MINORITY SUBCULTURES IN SCHOOLS

Ethnic minorities often form subcultures in school as a response to the racism and discrimination they experience in school. When individuals face bullying, marginalisation

1 Racism

or exclusion based on their ethnicity or race, they may seek refuge and solidarity within their own cultural or ethnic communities. These subcultures often serve as a means of support, identity affirmation and resilience against the challenges posed by racism in schools. Through shared experiences, language, traditions and values, ethnic minority students create spaces where they feel understood, respected and empowered. Unfortunately, there have been recent examples of when schools have been tone-deaf to such matters – for instance, the widely reported protests against a new uniform policy at a secondary school in Pimlico where new rules included a ban of Afro hairstyles in case they blocked the view of other students. These subcultures provide a sense of belonging and strength in numbers, as these children create a collective response to discrimination while also preserving and celebrating their cultures.

REFLECTION 1.2

Look at the Anti-bullying Alliance's *Racist and Faith Targeted Bullying: Top Tips for Schools* (link in resources below).

Which tips could your school work on to help address racist bullying?

Can you design an action plan, considering what resources and curriculum choices could be made to encourage a sense of belonging in school, including classroom and whole-school displays?

EFFECTIVE PRACTICES

Schools can prevent racism and exclusion by implementing various approaches that take on a school-wide approach to promote inclusivity, awareness and equity. Schools and universities should provide comprehensive anti-racism training for trainees, teachers and support staff during ITT, CPD and inset training sessions. This will equip them with the skills to recognise and address both explicit and subtle forms of racism.

Additionally, incorporating a diverse curriculum that reflects various cultures and histories can help all students feel valued and represented. Schools should also establish clear policies and procedures for reporting and addressing incidents of racism, ensuring that they are dealt with promptly and effectively, and should prioritise creating robust anti-racism and anti-bullying procedures. Encouraging open conversations about race and creating an environment where students can share their experiences without fear of retribution is also vitally important; anyone holding or sharing racist stereotypes should be challenged. Furthermore, schools should engage with parents and the wider community to build a supportive network that reinforces these values. By taking these steps, schools can create a more inclusive environment that minimises racism and prevents the exclusion of ethnic minority students.

Teachers need to be mindful to avoid tokenistic approaches. For instance, black history, which is widely adopted in many schools each October, has been criticised for not including UK black British history and being somewhat of a box-ticking exercise where figures and narratives from various ethnicities are not embedded across the history curriculum. Learning about black figures, such as Rosa Parks and Martin Luther King is valid, and their stories are often inspiring; however, simply including figures associated with the civil rights movement can lead to the misconception that historical figures of colour are only important in terms of their fight against oppression. This also leads to a further misconception that the fight for civil rights was fought and won historically rather than being an ongoing battle. To combat this, teachers should ensure that topics such as 'the Romans' should be taught in a way that conveys the ethnic diversity of the Roman Empire, thus normalising non-white narratives across the history national curriculum. Steps have been taken in diversifying the Key Stage 2 programme of study, with the mandatory topic of Non-European Civilisations; the DfE suggesting topics including ancient Islamic civilisation and the Shang Dynasty. Nevertheless, it can be all too easy to choose, when studying the Egyptians, to emphasise the role of British archaeologists, overriding the key message of North African advancement.

Schools also need to ensure visibility of all ethnic groups in everyday resources, such as picture books in reading areas. Even in recent decades, it has been found that, in some schools, the only pictures of black children in resources were in geography textbook passages on famine and lack of clean water. As a result, unhelpful stereotypes can be reinforced, again allowing misconceptions to occur where children think the whole continent of Africa is experiencing severe economic hardship where all children are ill and starving. With almost 20 per cent of the population in England and Wales (2021 Census) being non-white it is only right that a similar percentage of non-white ethnicities be visible in books, available resources such as PowerPoints and in the national curriculum. Meanwhile, teachers need to be proactive in developing their own subject knowledge, so they can avoid teaching in a way that perpetuates stereotypes of places and its people. In summary, inclusive education incorporates:

- inclusive policies that promote high outcomes for all students;

- a flexible and accommodative curriculum;

- strong and supportive leadership;

- equitable distribution of resources; and

- teachers who are trained in inclusive pedagogy and view it as their role to teach all learners in a diverse classroom (Schuelka, 2018).

1 Racism

REFLECTION 1.3

Download the National Education Union's *Anti-Racist Framework* (link in resources below). Use the self-audit checklists to see which elements, discussed above, are incorporated in your setting.

Which elements are you most 'on track' with?

Using the same document, can you relate to any of the barriers and myths explored on pages 7 and 8?

CASE STUDY 1.1

What effective practice looks like

Sarah, the head teacher of a primary school in Sunderland in the North East of England, returned from a conference on anti-racist education determined to make improvements at her own school by focusing on a more inclusive curriculum. Teaching in her region is a predominantly white profession with few children from other ethnic backgrounds. Sarah wanted to ensure her pupils had an appreciation of various cultures' contribution to history, music and art while also taking a more proactive stance against racist attitudes in the school community.

Sarah began mapping an inclusive curriculum, asking subject leads to identify areas of the curriculum which could be more broadly representative of various ethnicities. History, music, art and PSHE were identified as areas of the curriculum in which staff felt diversity could be readily embedded as a first step.

Art and PSHE leads felt that including more non-white artists and musicians, as well as examples of works from non-Western countries, was relatively easy to do.

The history lead felt the upper Key Stage topic of ancient Islamic civilisations would be a useful addition to the curriculum but felt they lacked subject knowledge. Sarah agreed to fund membership of the Historical Association so the teachers could engage with specific CPD to enable them to deliver the topic competently.

In Key Stage 1, the teacher felt researching a local significant figure of colour would be useful, particularly given the demographic of the school. Reaching out to the nearest heritage centre enabled the teacher to discover the story of Samuel Celestine Edwards, believed to be Britain's first black newspaper editor who spent time in Sunderland spreading an anti-racist message in the 1890s; some resources from the archives were used to support engaging delivery. During his research the teacher also discovered a new app which enables people to take part in a Black History Walk of Sunderland (see resources), so all pupils could take part in that during Black History Month. Sarah was aware of some of the controversies surrounding Black History Month; however, she felt that, having

12

embedded diversity throughout the curriculum, black history would not be tokenistic in her school, so she ring-fenced further teaching time to focus on the contributions of black individuals.

Looking at the diversity calendar she decided to celebrate World Interfaith Harmony Week, which could consolidate some of the anti-racist RE approaches the RE lead had researched through the National Association of Teachers of Religious Education (NATRE).

Sarah was also aware that many teachers lacked confidence in addressing and understanding issues surrounding racist bullying. Two websites had been recommended to her as having useful resources (details of these sites can be found in the further reading section of this chapter):

- Show Racism the Red Card

- UK Council for Child Internet Safety (UKCCIS).

Staff were asked to look at both websites and identify three things they had learnt or found useful at the website; these points formed the basis of a discussion at a staff meeting. Staff were then asked to identify how they had used what they had learnt in practice at a staff meeting four weeks later. All staff were also asked to contribute book ideas on a staff Padlet; each half term these would then be used – at first to create and then enhance an online inclusive virtual library resource that children and their families could access.

REFLECTION 1.4

Can you identify the positive steps Sarah took?

Look at the websites the staff at Sarah's school visited (links in resources below). How could you incorporate some of their resources into your own lessons?

Try creating a virtual library to be implemented in your school, use the Diverse and Inclusive section of Book for Topics (link in resources below) as a starting point to find inclusive books.

CONCLUSION

The DfE (2013) states how schools that: focus on providing equal opportunities for pupils of all cultural backgrounds; value diversity; challenge racism; provide safe and nurturing environments for their pupils; work closely with parents and the wider community; and focus on high achievement for all pupils are more successful in raising attainment in ethnic minorities groups. Yet, as this chapter has illustrated, various challenges exist and an equitable offer for children of all ethnicities is not available for all young people. However, the school environment can certainly make a difference, and teachers can have a positive impact by taking an anti-racist stance. Positive approaches include:

- teachers ostensibly showing support for cultural diversity, which has been found to lessen racist bullying as well as helping to embed diversity in the curriculum. Taking an 'anti-racist' rather than a 'non-racist' stance is a way of embracing this approach;

- schools setting, and demanding, high expectations for both teachers and students, with clear systems for targeting, tracking and monitoring of individual student progress;

- proactive monitoring by ethnicity to ensure all ethnic groups are achieving equally and to identify unexpected shortcomings in provision and target specific areas for attention. Monitoring also raises wider questions about setting, banding and exclusion processes.

CHAPTER SUMMARY

Within this chapter we have considered:

- what schools can do to assist children with different cultural backgrounds achieve their full potential;

- how teachers can help eradicate potential negative attitudes towards multiculturalism still existing in society today through constructive dialogue in the primary classrooms;

- showcase events outside school that may affect children from different cultural backgrounds in the school community;

- explore conscious and unconscious racial stereotypes and biases that may still influence teachers and learners' primary school experiences and how to address them.

FURTHER READING AND RESOURCES

Here are some groundbreaking books and resources to further your understanding of racism in education and wider society.

Anti-bullying Alliance *Racist and Faith Targeted Bullying: Top Tips for Schools*

https://anti-bullyingalliance.org.uk/tools-information/all-about-bullying/at-risk-groups/ racist-and-faith-targeted-bullying/racist-and

The Anti-bullying Alliance (ABA) has worked in partnership with the UKCCIS to produce the above tips to help schools begin to formulate a whole-school strategy to prevent and respond to race- and faith-targeted bullying. UKCCIS and ABA represent a broad range of charities, organisations and individuals committed to keeping children safe from bullying and abuse – both face to face and online.

National Education Union *Anti-Racist Framework* https://neu.org.uk/sites/default/files/2023-04/NEU2532%20Anti-racist%20framework%202022%20WEB%20v1.pdf

This framework is a response to the *Barriers* report (https://neu.org.uk/latest/library/barriers) which was based on the testimony of over 1,000 black teachers about the impact of racism in their workplaces. To address some of the concerns arising from that report, a framework was developed in consultation with the National Education Union (NEU) executive to help teachers develop anti-racist approaches in schools and workplaces. After further consultation and a pilot phase, this framework was launched in 2020 to help all schools and colleges in their work for just and inclusive education for children, young people and staff.

Show Racism the Red Card www.theredcard.org/

This is the UK's leading educational anti-racism charity, created specifically for teachers and educators. Here you will find free access to resources and step-by-step, guided lessons and activities so that you can promote anti-racism among the young people you work with.

UKCCIS Tackling_race_and_faith_targeted_bullying_face_to_face_and_online_-_a_guide.pdf

This is a guide for schools on tackling race- and faith-targeted bullying face to face and online. This guide highlights some key actions that can both prevent and respond to the issues in a school environment. There are also links to further resources and activities that can help you in your approach to promoting good relationships and equality in your school.

Books for Topics www.booksfortopics.com/

Diverse and Inclusive

The Good Immigrant, edited by Nikesh Shukla.
This book explores why immigrants come to the UK, why they stay and what it means to be 'other' in a country that doesn't seem to want you, doesn't truly accept you – however many generations you've been here – but still needs you for its diversity monitoring forms.

Me and White Supremacy, by Layla Saad
A book for you if you are interested in understanding how to dismantle the privilege within yourself so that you can stop (often unconsciously) inflicting damage on people of colour and, in turn, help other white people do better too.

1 Racism

Why I'm No Longer Talking to White People About Race, by Reni Eddo Lodge

This book sparked a national conversation by exploring everything from eradicated black history to the inextricable link between class and race. *Why I'm No Longer Talking to White People About Race* is the essential handbook if you want to understand race relations in Britain today.

Empireland: How Imperialism Has Shaped Modern Britain, by Sathnam Sanghera

This book offers a new critique of the history of the British Empire and its continuing impact on British society, drawing on secondary source material, personal experience and sharp enquiry.

Dispatches from the Diaspora: From Nelson Mandela to Black Lives Matter, by Gary Younge

'The past 30 years saw the end of apartheid, the election of Barack Obama and the foundation of the Black Lives Matter movement. Gary Younge has been there on the frontline throughout this time, translating history into words fused with truth, power and illumination.' David Lammy (UK Government Foreign Minister, 2024)

Black British Lives Matter: A Clarion Call for Equality, by Lenny Henry and Marcus Ryder

This book recognises black British experience within the Black Lives Matter movement through 19 prominent black figures, explaining why black lives should be celebrated when, too often, they are undervalued.

Brit(ish): On Race, Identity and Belonging, by Afua Hirsch

'This book is less a polemic about the past than an attempt to illuminate the problems of the present. This is a fierce, thought-provoking and fervent take on the most urgent questions facing us today.' Diana Evans (*Financial Times*)

The New Age of Empire: How Racism and Colonialism Still Rule the World, by Kehinde Andrews

This book offers no easy answers; an essential read to understand our profoundly corrupt global system.

This is Why I Resist: Don't Define My Black Identity, by Dr Shola Mos-Shogbamimu

This book builds on the anti-racism work that has come before and roots it firmly in our modern-day situation, especially following the Black Lives Matter movement of 2020. The book is not always comfortable to read, but it is necessary.

African and Caribbean People in Britain: A History, by Hakim Adi

This book explores the history of black people in Britain from earliest times – African presence pre-dates the Romans by almost 1,000 years – to the present day.

Broken Threads: My Family from Empire to Independence, by Mishal Husain

This book is an extraordinary family memoir from acclaimed newsreader and journalist, Mishal Husain, uncovering the story of her grandparents' lives amid empire, political upheaval and partition. The lives of Mishal Husain's grandparents changed forever in 1947, as the new nation states of India and Pakistan were born.

Hidden Heritage: Rediscovering Britain's Lost Love of the Orient, by Fatima Manji

This book explores the hidden stories which exist throughout Britain's galleries and museums, civic buildings and stately homes where relics can be found. They point to a more complex national history than is commonly remembered. These objects – lost, concealed or simply overlooked – expose the diversity of pre-20th-century Britain and the misconceptions around modern immigration narratives.

2

ECONOMIC INJUSTICE (CLASS, SOCIAL DEPRIVATION AND POVERTY)

LUCY DAVIES

— THIS CHAPTER

The chapter will provide opportunities for readers to reflect upon:

- activities at school where a child from a disadvantaged background may feel excluded
- how the hours from finishing school at 3pm to starting school again the next day might differ depending on socio-economic status (SES) and why the differences might impact achievement
- whether *class* still exists in the UK.

DEFINITIONS

To begin this chapter, we highlight some of the key terms and definitions that you may come across.

- *Free school meals* (FSMs): a statutory means-tested benefit that provides free school meals for children whose household income is below a certain level.

- *Pupil Premium* (PP): a government scheme that provides funding to schools to help support disadvantaged children.

- *Socio-economic status* (SES): an economic and sociological combined total measure of a person's work experience and of an individual's or family's access to economic resources and social position in relation to others.

INTRODUCTION

The Social Mobility Commission (2020) highlights persistent deprivation in various areas across England, where families face generational disadvantage, most often leading to disparities in social mobility. The report states that factors beyond education, such as local labour markets and family background, contribute to these disparities and states how regional leaders need to implement tailored programmes to improve social mobility and reduce deprivation caused by social class inequality.

This chapter will consider what is meant by SES, taking into account terms such as 'class' and 'social disadvantage'. Current and historical data will be used as evidence relating to SES effects on achievement to explore longitudinal relationships between the two factors. Despite government initiatives to close the attainment gap between children from economically disadvantaged backgrounds and their more affluent peers, recent research has highlighted that poverty still leads to segregation and underachievement in school (Gorard et al., 2021). Factors in a child's daily life which can affect learning that are linked to SES will be explored in relation to Maslow's hierarchy of needs, as well as the effectiveness of governmental and wider initiatives.

SOCIO-ECONOMIC STATUS AND ATTAINMENT

Studies investigating the link between socio-economic status and attainment are nothing new. While large-scale data sets provided by the Programme for International Student Assessment (PISA) show that many disadvantaged students can, and do, succeed at school (OECD, 2011), socio-economic status is associated with significant differences in performance in most countries and economies that participate in PISA.

It may then come as a surprise that socio-economic status is a not protected characteristic under the Equality Act (2010), given that it has such a strong association with a range of factors, including attainment levels. However, when looking at definitions of these terms we can begin to explore why. Socio-economic status is the combined measure of a family's social and economic status, taking into account their occupation, income and education level in the context of others in society. During a child's upbringing, their parents' occupation may change, their income may fluctuate and they may return to education. Socio-economic status therefore may change over time, unlike, for instance, a child's ethnicity. 'Social class' is a widely used term, but perhaps even more problematic to pindown, based on an individual's deemed socio-economic status and their subjective social status (APA, 2024). The UK has traditionally had a rigid class system stemming from the feudal system. Marrying outside one's class could have serious consequences, including disinheritance.

In modern times, divisions between classes have become more blurred and less rigid as society has moved towards meritocracy. An individual's perception of their own social class in comparison to others is known as subjective social status (Diemer et al., 2013). These blurred boundaries between classes can be explained by increased social mobility in society, a decline in industry and the raising of the age of compulsory education. A person's identification to a certain class is often based on their own interpreted cultural identity, which is more deep-rooted than simply their current income. Gorard and Saddiqui (2019) remind us that both socio-economic status and class remain and continue to be strong predetermining factors of how successful a child will be at school.

THE SCALE OF THE PROBLEM

In the year 2022–3, the Trussell Trust reported a sharp rise in food bank use and the number of children eligible for FSMs, which indicates the scale of financial difficulties that modern UK families are facing. Growing up in poverty impacts children for life. Children who grow up in poverty go on to obtain fewer GCSEs, to work fewer hours and to earn less. In addition, children who grow up in poverty are likely to live fewer years and in less good physical and mental health than their peers (Joseph Rowntree Foundation, 2024). Teachers and schools are therefore faced with both practical and emotional challenges in supporting an ever-growing number of children from economically disadvantaged backgrounds.

LEARNING RESOURCE 2.1

- UNICEF's 2007 report placed the UK last out of 21 countries based on children's overall welfare, considering factors such as material wealth, housing and education. Despite moving up the rankings in subsequent international comparisons, child poverty and welfare remain a widespread issue.

- Approximately 4.2 million children are living in poverty in the UK, which equates to almost a third of learners (29 per cent) (Action for Children, 2024).

THE ATTAINMENT GAP

Socio-economic status has been a pervasive influencing factor in the educational success, or lack thereof, of children for centuries, let alone decades. For those of you who have researched your family tree, you may have already discovered that some of your 19th-century ancestors from a working-class background signed marriage certificates with a 'X', as illiteracy rates during the 1800s were high (Ingleby, 2021). Unfortunately, research suggests that even today 16.4 per cent of adults in England are estimated to have very low literacy, which means they may struggle with longer texts and unfamiliar topics (OECD, 2011). Of course, positive steps have been taken in improving the general level of education across society through a widening of access to free education and raising the compulsory school-leaving age (discussed later in this chapter). Yet, two stark facts remain. Firstly, children from economically disadvantaged backgrounds continue to underperform academically when examining standardised test results. The Sutton Trust (2021) found children who have FSMs for over 80 per cent of their schooling had a learning gap of 22.7 months by the time they left school. Secondly, when children and young adults are not able access to high-quality teaching and learning they can be vulnerable to a lack of social inclusion (Services for Education, 2024).

ATTAINMENT AT EARLY YEARS AND KEY STAGE 1

The Early Years Foundation Stage framework (gov.uk, 2023b) is designed so that children can meet 17 Early Learning Goals across seven areas of learning by the end of Reception. As Figure 2.1 shows, there are consistently fewer children who are eligible for FSMs meeting the Early Learning Goals across all 17 areas of the curriculum than children who are not eligible for FSMs.

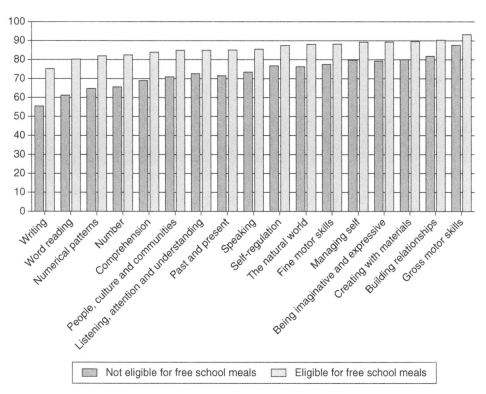

Figure 2.1 Percentage of children at the expected level by Early Learning Goal and eligibility for FSM 2022/23 (data source: gov.uk, 2023a)

PRIMARY SCHOOL

Perhaps unsurprisingly, given the gap that has already emerged by the end of Reception, economic disadvantage continues to have a negative impact on children throughout their primary education. Year 6 SATS tests, compulsory at all state-maintained primary schools, give a reliable insight into attainment and progress for all pupils. Some figures from the DfE (gov.uk, 2023a) appear to indicate that children from economically disadvantaged backgrounds are making more progress year on year:

- 41 per cent of disadvantaged pupils achieved the expected standard in all three subjects in 2023 (up from 38 per cent in 2022);

- 62 per cent of pupils achieved the expected standard in all three subjects in 2023 (up from 59 per cent in 2022).

However, compared to classmates who are not eligible for FSMs, they not only remain less likely to attain high scores in SATS, but the gap is widening, as shown in Table 2.1.

Table 2.1   Percentage of pupils reaching the expected standard for reading, writing and mathematics

	2022	2023	Change
Not eligible for FSM	59.3	61.9	2.6
Eligible for FSM	38.4	40.8	2.4
Attainment gap	20.9	21.1	0.2

SECONDARY SCHOOL AND BEYOND

As children move through secondary school the attainment gap continues to widen. By the time children from economically disadvantaged backgrounds finish their GCSEs they are approximately 18 months behind their more affluent peers (Hutchings, 2021). Numerous stark statistics exist illustrating the gap at secondary school:

- pupils eligible for FSMs gain an average of 243 points (in GCSE and equivalent qualifications) compared to 319 for non-eligible pupils;

- 75 per cent of non-FSM children pass both English and Mathematics GCSEs compared to 47 per cent of FSM children (gov.uk, 2023a).

For children from economically disadvantaged backgrounds who achieve academically and go on to study at university, it seems their family income level may still affect their access to the same experience as others. At age 25 years, 23.0 per cent of FSM recipients who attended school in England had recorded earnings above the annualised full-time equivalent of the Living Wage in comparison with 43.5 per cent of those that did not.

HISTORICAL SOCIO-ECONOMIC INEQUALITIES

Using data from PISA, the OECD has concluded that: 'while many disadvantaged students succeed at school … socioeconomic status is associated with significant differences in performance in most countries and economies that participate in PISA. Advantaged students tend to outscore their disadvantaged peers by large margins' (Clarke et al., 2022). The strength of the relationship varies from very strong to moderate across participating countries, but the relationship does exist in each country.

The inequalities in educational outcomes and school belongingness more broadly have been stubbornly persistent and not just confined to the UK. In 1966, the US-based Coleman Report found that schools themselves did little to affect a student's academic outcomes over and above what the students themselves brought with them to school: 'the inequalities imposed on children by their home, neighbourhood and peer environment are carried along to become the inequalities with which they confront adult life at the end of school' (p. 325). Despite being almost 50 years old, Coleman's findings align closely with more recent conclusions drawn by Gorard and Siddiqui (2019), who point out that a variety of complex issues are involved in explaining the effect size of socio-economic status and attainment – such as talent, motivation and a 'learner identity' – which may play a role in creating these gaps.

Having said that, schools or, more precisely, educational structures do seem to have played a part in perpetuating, if not necessarily causing the academic attainment gap. Free education for all primary-aged children was established under the 1891 Elementary Education Act; with the passing of the Elementary Education Act (school attendance) Act two years later, the compulsory school-leaving age was raised to 11. Even after this, children from working-class families often had sporadic school attendance as many were also required to work to contribute to the household income. In contrast, for wealthy families fee-paying schools and universities were already well-established by this point.

The next major piece of legislation was the 1944 Education Act which created three types of state-funded schools known as the *tripartite system*. The creation of grammar schools, secondary modern schools and technical schools was seen as a way of ensuring children were prepared for their likely occupation through a secondary education which was most suited to their academic ability (measured by the '11-plus' test). This scheme was not without controversy and an argument against the system was that children were being categorised into a type of school that could limit their later career path based on the 11-plus test.

PHYSIOLOGICAL AND SAFETY RISKS FOR POVERTY AT HOME

Let us consider the potential variation in experiences of children from economically disadvantaged background compared to their more affluent peers before the first lesson of the day has even begun.

2 Economic injustice

CASE STUDY 2.1

Variation in children's experiences of schools

A child who is eligible for FSMs is one of the 2 million children in the UK living (one in five) in overcrowded, unaffordable or inadequate houses (National Housing Federation, 2021). Their morning routine may be detrimentally affected by a disrupted journey to school reliant on public transport or, if that is not affordable, a long walk in bad weather. By the time they get to school, they may have already been out of the house for some time, possibly in wet conditions. Their clothing may be less than ideal as their parents cannot afford to replace a lost rain jacket or holey shoes. The child is already tired from lack of sleep caused by poor living conditions and, like many other children in the UK affected by mould and dampness, is suffering from the effects of asthma brought on by these conditions. Although the school has a free breakfast club, the cereal provided does not satisfy the child who did not have a substantial meal the previous evening. And while the school has a second-hand uniform box in Reception for parents to access, the economic situation at home means that the child's parents cannot afford the washing powder to use at a laundrette, let alone the price of a washing machine and its associated running costs, so the child has to pluck up the courage to tell the teacher they have not bought their PE kit – again.

Meanwhile, their comfortably off friends may enjoy a little longer in bed in their own neatly decorated, warm bedroom. They will get taken to school in one of their parent's cars, meaning they don't have to rush to leave the house as a direct drive only takes ten minutes. Although there is a short walk from the car to the school's gates, they have a substantial coat with a hood that helps them brave the elements. They're looking forward to PE as they've been going to gymnastics club twice a week and are feeling confident about showing off their cartwheels later in the day.

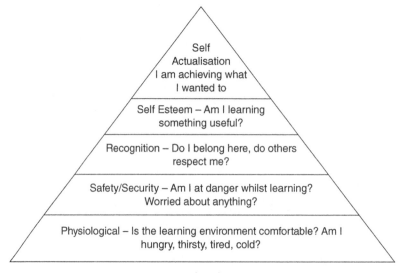

Figure 2.2   Maslow's (1943) hierarchy of needs expressed in educational terms

Comparing these two experiences in relation to Maslow's well-known hierarchy of needs model (see Figure 2.2) it is clear that the first child is not having their physiological needs met. Children from economically disadvantaged backgrounds may not only have poor sleep, but also may have concerns stemming from uncertainty about finances. In turn these children are between two and three times more likely to be living in a family where a member will develop a mental health condition (Safran et al., 2009; Reiss, 2013). According to Maslow's model, their ability to then self-motivate at school is seriously impeded.

THE COVID-19 PANDEMIC

This chapter has already highlighted how children from economically disadvantaged backgrounds consistently achieve less highly than their peers from wealthier backgrounds. The Covid-19 pandemic caused more visible unequal disruption to children's learning, with detailed SATs result reports, released by the DfE in 2022, unveiling the national decline in results across the country, widening the attainment gap as children from economically disadvantaged backgrounds fell even further behind than their better-off peers. Looking at the figures more closely, in 2023, only 43 per cent of these children (those on FSMs or in care, making up a third of children taking SATs) reached the attainment targets, compared to 65 per cent of non-disadvantaged pupils, widening the attainment gap to the greatest it has been since 2012. Officials from the Department for Education (DfE) have cautioned that the impact of Covid-19 has caused the attainment gap to widen by approximately 75 per cent, marking a reversal in the previous trend where the gap seemed to be decreasing. This paints a concerning picture for social mobility in the UK, as children from economically disadvantaged backgrounds have less and less of a chance of achieving that upward mobility required to break through the long-existing social class barriers.

SO WHY HAS THE COVID-19 PANDEMIC CAUSED SUCH A GREAT DECLINE IN ACADEMIC PROGRESS?

Attending school is the most effective way for children to build their skills and increase their chances of becoming socially mobile. Dräger et al. (2023) explain how even a relatively short disruption to a child's time in school can severely hinder their academic progress and development of social skills, due to lack of teacher-led lessons and peer interactions. Although families are vital to a child's education through complementing the teaching a child receives at school, during the pandemic, when families were often educating children at home with support from online materials, there is no doubt that progress started to fall (EEF, 2021). Children continued their education at home, posing issues for parents – who suddenly had to balance their own working lives, family life and access to technology and assist with online learning. Of course, all parents would have experienced this differently, but disadvantaged families certainly experienced hardship.

The pandemic has undeniably brought to light and exacerbated educational inequalities, particularly between students attending state-funded schools and those in independent schools. Independent schools, which primarily educate children from higher socio-economic backgrounds, generally provided their students with more consistent access to tablets and computers for online schoolwork during the pandemic. Additionally, these schools were able to offer more comprehensive online teaching, thanks to their greater plethora of resources and smaller class sizes.

In contrast to this, students in state schools come from more diverse socio-economic back-grounds, with a significant number coming from low-income households. Families may have lacked the technology or stationery required for children to complete their online assignments. Pupils from state schools were less likely to receive satisfactory online teach-ing (Understanding Society, 2020), a concerning trend given that the state sector serves a substantial number of disadvantaged children, especially as the attainment gap had already started to widen since 2019. The government's definition of 'disadvantaged' pupils includes those eligible for the Pupil Premium and those deemed 'vulnerable', such as those with an education, health and care (EHC) plan, a social worker, or those assessed by local authorities as otherwise vulnerable. Children in these groups face disproportionately disrupted access to education even under normal circumstances and struggled to access suitable online resources and teaching during lockdown.

Additionally, the lockdown restrictions for leaving the house, the closing of libraries and museums – public places for learning – during and since the pandemic have also con-tributed to the slowing of academic progress, leaving families unable to access learning opportunities outside the home. This is especially ostracising for disadvantaged families who may have previously relied on public libraries and museums for access to technology and reading materials.

Since the end of the Covid-19 pandemic, the UK has entered an economic crisis, com-monly known as the *cost-of-living crisis*. The cost of everything has increased, leaving all families – but especially disadvantaged families – in an even worse financial position. The impact of the cost-of-living crisis has compounded the academic downturn caused by the Covid-19 pandemic; the consequences this has had on education cannot be under-estimated, as families are now facing money worries, mental health struggles and lack of access to technology. Families who might have already been struggling to make ends meet may now have to prioritise paying bills and buying food and household essentials, rather than paying for technology and school supplies. Furthermore, the cost-of-living crisis has severely impacted school budgets. The increasing cost of school resources, such as tech-nology and stationery, are bound to limit what schools can feasibly afford. Many teachers across the country already feel compelled to spend their own money on school resources, but the cost-of-living crisis will no doubt reduce the number of teachers who are willing to pay for resources out of their own pockets. Since the pandemic, as highlighted by the decline in academic progress, particularly with SATs results, disadvantaged children need more and more support in school from teaching assistants (TAs) and interventions, putting greater pressure on school funding.

Schools are urgently inputting cost-saving measures to combat the rising costs, which is no doubt severely impacting the school learning environment, hindering the progress and development of all children, especially those from disadvantaged backgrounds who have already fallen so much further behind during the pandemic compared to their more well-off peers. Schools have had to make cuts to their staffing, stripping away TAs, one-to-one help and intervention opportunities; 47 per cent of primary schools have had to cut TA numbers and hours. Due to rising costs and inflation, schools have also had to cut out aspects of the curriculum and cut back on school trips, enrichment activities and essential supplies, such as stationery and technology (*Schools Week*, 2024). This means that children who struggle to access such resources and activities outside school are less likely to make use of enriching resources and participate in cultural and educational experiences outside the classroom, which help to embed previously learned knowledge, create new learning memories and help children to become well-rounded, cultured individuals.

As the government closed schools during the first lockdown, school attendance from all children dramatically dropped, with the proportion of vulnerable pupils (who are more likely to be from economically disadvantaged backgrounds) attending school being approximately 15 per cent. Some children from economically disadvantaged backgrounds who attended school under *key worker care* had similar provisions to children who were learning from home. However, in reality, many schools had teachers working in rotation, many relied heavily on TA-led lessons, classes were merged, children may have attended school part-time and 29 per cent of primary schools focused on providing extra-curricular activities, rather than teaching the curriculum (as opposed to 17 per cent in schools with the lowest levels of deprivation). Therefore, even though children attending school may have had better access to teachers, technology and resources, they were still held back from making progress by the provisions schools put in place to manage lockdown learning. Consequently, many prior gaps in learning will not have been addressed, causing the average attainment of all children to drop, but especially that of deprived children – which plummeted even further.

Problems also arose for children attempting home learning, especially for those from more economically disadvantaged backgrounds, as many children may not have attended many online lessons, potentially due to a lack of access to suitable technology, due to sharing among family members, lack of quiet space to work or other more serious family issues. The Children's Commissioner also observed how many of the children who may be vulnerable in society, who would have benefitted from attending school during lockdown, did not attend during those years due to not being 'listed' as

2 Economic injustice

vulnerable. Therefore, many children learning from unrecognised vulnerable homes were not only denied the education that 'listed' vulnerable children could access, but also the crucial safety of being in a school setting.

CASE STUDY 2.2

Kate

Kate, the head teacher of a junior school in Brighton and Hove, noticed that children coming up from the infants' school did not seem as confident and socially mature as they had done before the pandemic. Teachers raised concerns about the lack of resilience many of the children showed in lessons, particularly in activities like problem-solving in mathematics or drafting longer pieces of writing. Meanwhile, the dexterity of the children also seemed to have fallen. Having spoken to other head teachers, Kate felt offering enjoyable extra-curricular activities that would give children opportunities to work with peers and be physically beneficial, progressing their gross and fine-motor skills could help.

However, Kate was aware that there was already a pattern in her school which showed a gap in attainment between the children eligible for FSMs and the non-FSM children. Kate wanted to ensure that the extra-curricular activities opportunities she offered would be accessible for all pupils and not only those who could afford to pay.

Kate used the Child Poverty Action Group website (see below) for support and found that holiday clubs could also help reduce the attainment gap and also provide informal opportunities for 'Covid catch-up'. For the first year, Kate decided that the summer holiday would be the ideal time for camp, with it being an extended time away from school. Kate approached the Holiday and Food programme (HAF) for funding, logistical support and advice. Younger siblings were also able to attend, as were non-FSM pupils, providing they paid a small amount towards the camp.

During the camp, children were able to enjoy arts and crafts, as well as sports activities like short tennis, tag rugby and cricket. Kate was pleased that many of the activities were ones that could be carried forward into lunch-time or after-school clubs once the new academic year began.

REFLECTION 2.1

Kate used the *Tackling Child Poverty: A Guide for Schools* from Child Poverty Action Group (CPAG, 2020) (link below) to help with her Holiday Club Plan. In the document, a need for having clear outcomes is identified. What are some outcomes/aims you would like to achieve in your school?

What steps will you need to take to achieve these outcomes?

POVERTY-PROOFING THE SCHOOL DAY

During post-pandemic times, there are greater opportunities to lessen the inequalities for children from economically disadvantaged backgrounds that were exposed during school closures. Although income is not a protected characteristic under 2010's Equality Act, schools are expected to ensure the socio-economic background of their pupils does not affect their access to all aspects of their education. No activity or planned activity in schools should identify, exclude, treat differently or make assumptions about those children whose household income or resources are lower than others. But how can this be done? Research conducted by Newcastle University (Mazzolli Smith and Todd, 2019) claims various factors can support an equitable offer:

- food and FSMs

- resources

- homework

- uniform

- extra-curricular activity

- charity, community and fundraising

- celebrations

- bullying.

LEADERSHIP AND GOVERNANCE

Some areas have already begun to implement poverty-proofing across their schools. Table 2.2 considers each of these factors, giving an exemplification of how inequality can be highlighted; it then suggests ways this inequity could be mitigated. These are some of the measures which have been implemented in infants and junior schools in the North East of England.

GOVERNMENT INITIATIVES

The UK government is constantly under pressure to make positive changes to the education system to improve academic outcomes for all children and increase the chances of achieving social mobility for children from economically disadvantaged backgrounds. As explored earlier in the chapter, various initiatives have come and gone (and sometimes returned in a slightly different guise). The previous administration's introduction of the Pupil Premium was undoubtedly its most significant initiative to help close the attainment gap. The Pupil Premium was introduced to improve educational outcomes for children from economically

2 Economic injustice

disadvantaged backgrounds attending state-maintained schools. The cost of Pupil Premium for the 2023–4 academic year was estimated at £2.9 billion.

During the Covid-19 pandemic Universal Credit payments were temporarily increased by £20 a week; this increase has been identified as a major contributing factor to 400,000 children being 'pulled out of poverty' (Action for Children, 2024). However, once this was rolled back in October 2021, poverty levels quickly rose again, meaning that current child poverty levels remain similar to those before the pandemic.

Table 2.2 Poverty-proofing the school day

	Potential for inequality	**Suggestions for best practice**
Resources	Children are asked to bring in ingredients for a food technology lesson. Some parents/carers may struggle to buy these, and the pupil is then unable to take part in the lesson and their exclusion is obvious to classmates.	Ask for donations of ingredients at the start of the year, as the quantities are more likely to be able to be shared out between several pupils.
Homework	Homework projects which involve documenting what children have done in their time off school can be difficult for children to complete if they have not had the opportunity to go anywhere; having limited stationery resources can also be a hindrance.	Give all children the same resources to complete; instead of a holiday diary, which requires a short amount of text and some illustrations, give children a comic template. Provide simple stationery packs to children. If possible, consider a summer camp at the school where children can engage in fun and educational activities for a small fee or free if the child is eligible for FSM or at the head teacher's discretion.
Uniform	Branded clothing bought at specific uniform shops is more expensive and means some parents may only be able to afford one of each item. With the cost of washing clothes also being a factor to consider, this can lead to children having to wear the same item all week, meaning some disadvantaged children to be dressed in worn, dirty clothes.	Opt for non-branded shirts/ polo shirts, sweatshirts and shorts, trousers or dresses for both the main uniform and PE kit. Have a donation point at Reception for recycled/upcycled uniforms which all families can have access to, should they need new uniforms without the economic cost associated with them.

	Potential for inequality	Suggestions for best practice
Clubs	Many children miss out on extra-curricular activities outside school, like sports clubs, due to the money involved to buy kit, transport to training, etc.	Discuss after-school club ideas at a staff meeting in advance of the school year; after-school clubs should be meaningful and replicate the types of opportunities out-of-school organisations can offer. Network with local charities, sports and arts groups to try and enrich what the school can offer.
Celebrations/ special days	Events like World Book Day can put parents/carers under pressure if schools want children to dress as a book character. Similarly, raising money for local or national charities where the teacher collects donations by going around the class asking pupils can be embarrassing for children who have not been able to bring in a cash donation.	Children can create masks of their favourite book character the day before World Book Day while at school. A donation box could be put at the front of the class, with children asked to post their coin at some point through the day, so it makes it less obvious who has and has not donated.

THE ROLE OF ITT PROVIDERS

As this chapter has demonstrated, disparities between children of different socio-economic status have long been identified. Various attempts have been made to support children from less affluent backgrounds, but data shows that there is a persistent attainment gap. Access to the same standard of education is not a fix-all solution as illustrated by older learners' responses to social inclusion surveys in higher education. While, on the one hand, the Pupil Premium fund may have had an impact, it is not without its problems, as discussed previously. In addition, a reliance on government-led initiatives can be problematic, as a change of government often leads to changes to schemes as well. On the other hand, school-led approaches, such as those advocated by the Poverty-Proofing the School Day initiatives, give school staff more control of their approaches, thus mitigating the changeable nature of government schemes.

However, some schools are more advanced than others in implementation of poverty-proofing. Depending on the socio-economic demographic area of the ITT provider, as well as trainees' own background, knowledge of the effects of socio-economic status and school experience (including attainment) can mean teachers gaining newly qualified teacher status (QTS) can enter the profession with varied levels of both understanding and first-hand experience in the classroom of supporting children from economically disadvantaged backgrounds. Some trainees, for instance, may have had placements at two schools where one school may have had a higher proportion of children eligible for FSMs and where the school has already begun working on poverty-proofing measures. Meanwhile, another trainee may have had placements based in more affluent locations where very few children were eligible for FSMs. While the *ITT Core Content Framework* (CCF; DfE, 2019) demands providers encourage adaptive teaching there is no specific mention of children from economically disadvantaged backgrounds.

ITT courses offer the opportunity to support those entering the career to think about poverty-proofing their own classrooms once they have gained QTS. We suggest providers:

- think about providing opportunities for trainees to share ideas from different placement schools; share experiences from own schooling; bring together practices from various parts of England and further afield to develop an awareness that approaches vary widely within schools; and learn from examples of best practice;

- deliver specific sessions on socio-economic disadvantage and class as part of meeting the *adaptive teaching* requirements of the CCF to help address social stigma and misconceptions surrounding low-income households;

- ensure trainees understand the complex nature of socio-economic conditions and social class and how other factors such as ethnicity can influence attainment levels of a child entitled to FSMs;

- improve trainees' confidence in working in areas of higher-than-average socio-economic deprivation.

The aim of providers should be to empower their trainees to help tackle economic injustice and not shy away from applying to, and staying at, schools with higher-than-average levels of FSM pupils. Longer term, this could reduce SES segregation between schools, but this can also act to deter more qualified teachers from working in heavily disadvantaged schools (Copeland, 2018).

CONCLUSION

This chapter has shown that socio-economic disadvantage is a stubbornly persistent problem. While class (and classist) attitudes may still exist they do so in a less pervasive way than in previous years, which is a positive step forward. Meanwhile, some initiatives do appear to benefit children from economically disadvantaged backgrounds. However, the disadvantage gap is increasing more rapidly than progress being made by FSM children. There are also children who are in economic hardship but whose families do not meet the threshold for benefits. Poverty-proofing the school day is an effective way to mitigate inequality for children from economically disadvantaged backgrounds, whether they are eligible for FSMs or not. An awareness of the disadvantage gap and a genuine understanding of why income causes both academic and more holistic challenges for children is needed by all in the teaching profession, from trainee teachers to head teachers.

CHAPTER SUMMARY

Within this chapter we have considered:

- the meaning and measurement of socio-economic status;
- home-life factors which can be associated with lower SES and affect academic potential being fully realised;
- social mobility and initiatives in place to help social mobility;
- what can teachers and schools do to provide an equitable approach to ensure SES is not a barrier to success for any child.

FURTHER READING AND RESOURCES

Stephen Gorard, Nadia Siddiqui and Beng Huat See (2019) The difficulties of judging what difference the Pupil Premium has made to school intakes and outcomes in England. *Research Papers in Education, 36*(3), 355–79. https://doi.org/10.1080/02671522.2019.1677759

Child Poverty Action Group (CPAG) *Cost of the School Day Toolkit – Scotland.* https://cpag.org.uk/what-we-do/project-work/cost-school-day/resources/toolkits/toolkit-scotland
CPAG has designed a useful toolkit designed to get everyone talking about the cost of the school day.

Child Poverty Action Group (CPAG) (2020) *Tackling Child Poverty: A Guide for Schools*
This is the document referred to in Case study 2.2 that provides further examples of how schools have implemented successful initiatives.
https://cpag.org.uk/sites/default/files/2023-08/Tackling%20child%20poverty-%20a%20guide%20for%20schools.pdf

THE HOLIDAY AND FOOD ACTIVITY PROGRAMME

www.gov.uk/government/publications/holiday-activities-and-food-programme/holiday-activites-and-food-programme-2024

2 Economic injustice

This is the link to the programme mentioned in Case study 2.2 that provides a scheme for providers wishing to set up holiday provision.

SUTTON TRUST

www.suttontrust.com/
The Sutton Trust is an educational charity which aims to support social mobility and address disadvantage. It contains a variety of studies which can help educators make choices about how to support children from economically disadvantaged backgrounds.

3
GENDER DISCRIMINATION AND SEXISM IN SCHOOLS

GEORGIA VENESS

THIS CHAPTER

The chapter will provide opportunities for readers to reflect upon:

- curriculum areas which might lend themselves to promoting gender equality
- challenges faced by teachers and learners relating to sex and gender
- observable differences between boys and girls, such as attainment gaps and subject choice at A-level (and implications for primary practitioners).

DEFINITIONS

To begin this chapter, we highlight some of the key terms and definitions that you may come across:

- *Gender*: for the purpose of this chapter, gender refers to the socially constructed characteristics of men and women, and boys and girls.
- *Sex*: refers to the biological differences between males and females and is assigned at birth.

INTRODUCTION

Various policy developments aimed at equal rights for woman have been implemented in modern times, from the 1975 Sex Discrimination Act to the Equality Act of 2010. Despite such legislation, a gender divide can still be seen in educational settings, as well as in wider society, with women's contributions being overlooked. This chapter acknowledges the argument from Gurian and Stevens (2005) that biological factors influence some of the differences we see between boys and girls in the classroom. However, it also examines how factors such as societal gender stereotypes and language can influence children's behaviours and expectations at home and at school. This chapter provides insight into what gender differences look like in schools and what teachers can do to ensure sex and gender equality in the classroom.

ROLE OF GENDER DURING PRIMARY SOCIALISATION

Children first learn about gender during primary socialisation, which is the process where children learn the norms, values and behaviours that society expects of them. It is during these early years that children start to learn that different expectations are placed on boys and girls. Gender is socially constructed through the exposure to norms, behaviours and gendered roles that are associated with the gender and sex somebody is assigned at birth. For example, in the majority of cultures across the world, men are often seen as more aggressive and protective than their female counterparts, who are more often viewed as being more passive and nurturing. The gender roles, men and women that we recognise in the UK today may have a biological underpinning, although thoughts that they are an after-effect of men hunting and women nurturing in ancient times are no longer thought to be accurate. Though gender roles have evolved over time, the biological element of reproduction still separates the roles of men and women in society today, raising the question of whether gender roles are biologically innate or socially constructed. It is important to note that the social constructs of gender differ from culture to culture and that they can also change over time. For example, the colour pink used to be associated with men and boys as it represented vigour and was seen as more aggressive; however, the colour pink is now associated with being feminine, as suggested by Uncu et al (2018). Furthermore, groundbreaking research from Mead (1935) unveiled the disparity in how different cultures view gender and the roles and behaviours associated with it. Mead was an anthropologist who set out to study tribes in Papua New Guinea with the aim of discovering whether gendered behaviours were innate or socially constructed. Mead found vast differences in gender roles and behaviours between the different tribes, separating biologically based sex from socially constructed gender. Table 3.1 zooms in on how differently gender was displayed from tribe to tribe and exhibits how gender roles differ between societies.

Table 3.1   Gendered behaviours according to tribes

Tribe name	Gendered behaviours exhibited
Arapesh tribe	Both males and females displayed a gentle temperament
Mundugumor (now Biwat) tribe	Both males and females were violent and aggressive
Tchambuli (now Chambri) tribe	Females displayed dominance and power over the males while the males presented as being more emotionally dependent

Although biological sex assigned at birth plays its role in the creation of gender roles, Mead's findings clearly highlight how society also plays its part in constructing and shaping the socially acceptable roles and more normalised behaviours of men and women.

Oakley (2005), who is renowned for her poignant research into gender roles – specifically how boys and girls are socialised to act differently during primary socialisation – suggested that parents teach their boys to be masculine and girls to be feminine in four main ways. We acknowledge that this research is dated and uses the terms 'male and female', which refers to the sex assigned to someone at birth, rather than using 'men and women'; the following table is useful in understanding how parents/carers may inadvertently guide their children towards different gender roles.

Table 3.2   Parental approach to different gender roles

Name of process	Manipulation	Canalisation	Gendered activities	Verbal appellations
Definition	The process of parents manipulating their children into behaving differently	The process of parents directing their children to gendered objects	The process of parents guiding children towards activities associated with each gender	The process of parents giving their children gendered nicknames
Examples	• Holding baby girls more tenderly, compared to perhaps bouncing a baby boy on their knee • Spending more time attending to the appearance of girls and dressing them in feminine clothes and dressing boys in more masculine clothes	• Directing girls towards more feminine toys that are centred around housework or being a mother, such as dolls and pretend domestic appliances • Encouraging boys to play with more masculine toys that are associated with manual labour and STEM activities, such as toolkits, building bricks and science experiment kits	• Encouraging girls to go to a ballet or gymnastics class, as well as take on household chores • Sending boys to play football or rugby or partake in more risk-taking activities such as camping, climbing or going to adventure playgrounds	• Parents giving their baby girl nicknames such as 'princess' and being more likely to call a girl 'beautiful' or 'pretty', commenting on her physical appearance • Calling boys 'brave' or 'like a soldier' when they are praised for being tough or masculine

3 Gender discrimination and sexism in schools

REFLECTION 3.1

As a teacher have you noticed gender roles being established in your classroom or school setting without being consciously recognised? Does your school take measures to actively address these issues?

HOW DO ADULTS REINFORCE GENDER STEREOTYPES?

Oakley's (2005) research can help us to understand how gender is socialised from an early age and how differences in the way girls and boys are expected to behave becomes apparent to children in the very early years of their lives. As a child joins nursery or primary school in the Early Years, Oakley's four processes of gender socialisation still very much do their part to guide children into gender roles in these settings. Toys that children are provided with play a vital role in shaping a child's development by affecting what skills they learn, what interests they develop and also how they view themselves. A experiment by the BBC (www.bbc.co.uk/programmes/p05cfsym) which explored gendered toys is useful in displaying how adults can guide children to play with different toys depending on whether they are a boy or a girl. The study concluded that the majority of the time, if a girl was dressed as a boy, the adult would choose a stereotypical *boys'* toy for them to play with and vice versa.

A similar study conducted by New York University and Arizona State University (Davis and Hines, 2020) found that toy preferences are not necessarily innate, by concluding that a third of the time the boys in the study chose to play with a stereotypical *girls'* toy more often than the girls did. Similarly, boys' toys were picked by girls more often than boys. This links back to Oakley's research, specifically the process of *canalisation*, clearly showing how toy preferences have been socially constructed and how misguided society has been about what these preferences actually are – as, of course, they will be different for each child, irrespective of their gender. This study also provides food for thought on how these ideas about toy stereotypes become embedded as children get older and how children often feel like they have to play with toys more often associated with their gender to avoid bullying or discrimination.

A study conducted by YouGov (2017) investigated how adults would feel buying a stereotypical boys' toy for a girl and vice versa. The study found that 42 per cent of the people who took part in the study would feel comfortable buying a girl a boys' toy. More interestingly, only 31 per cent of people reported feeling comfortable buying a boy a girls' toy, highlighting how it is less socially acceptable for a boy to play with a girls' toy. The findings from this study demonstrate how firmly gender stereotypes are embedded in society. Feminist movements have worked hard to empower girls and women to cross gender boundaries to play with more 'masculine' toys and enjoy activities that are more traditionally associated with boys, such as football, engineering and video gaming. Helping girls

38

engage with more typically masculine activities can help them to find interests and develop skills in these areas. Women role models such as the Lionesses (the women's England football team) have also helped to show that women and girls can cross the limitations applied to them based on their gender and succeed in areas more typically associated with men and boys. However, crossing these gender boundaries is not as easy for boys. Research from Narsaria (2019) suggests that the boundaries of girls' and boys' toys are less concrete for girls than boys, with the latter more likely to be criticised for playing with a girls' toy. It seems that boys have less freedom to choose what toys they want to play with without being teased or bullied for it. Parents also are less likely to be pleased about their sons playing with more feminine toys than they would be about their girls playing with more masculine toys (Narsaria, 2019). So, while a lot of people believe that girls and women are more subject to – and limited by – gender stereotypes, there are many ways in which patriarchal pressures also place limits on boys and men, such as the gendered expectations to be strong rather than nurturing, and logical rather than creative.

Changing attitudes have caused a shift in parenting techniques, as more parents are recently reporting that they avoid gender-stereotyped toys and allow children to choose their own toys more freely. Martinez (2022) explains how these parents are contributing towards a gender revolution as they try to break the negative implications of gender binary stereotypes by removing gender stereotypes from the early socialisation of their children. These parents may opt to dress their children in and paint their bedrooms in more gender-neutral colours to try and reduce some of the gender stereotypes that have been normalised over many years.

The website Not only Pink and Blue (updated 2024) has some impressive information and resources to help parents and teachers challenge the stereotypes associated with gendered toys and activities.

REFLECTION 3.2

As a teacher what can you do to break down gender stereotypes that tend to become embedded in Early Years settings particularly? What strategies could you use as a teacher?

IMPACT OF GENDER ROLES AND BEHAVIOURS ON EDUCATIONAL OUTCOMES

The patterns of behaviour that children learn in the Early Years follow them through school and become more and more embedded the older they get. Socialisation in the Early Years plays a huge part in the creation of a child's identity, including their likes and dislikes and how they view themselves and their abilities.

Research from Pope (2015) argues that children develop different cognitive abilities depending on the toys they play with from a young age. Boys' toys promote mathematical and scientific thinking, whereas girls' toys are more likely to develop their verbal and linguistic skills. The skills developed affect a child throughout their lifetimes as they affect a child's academic attainment (gender differences in educational outcomes will be discussed later in the chapter), subject choices for GCSEs and A-levels and also university and career choices. Pope's study concludes that it is 'imperative that more children engage in cross-gender toy play in order to foster a wider range of skills suitable towards a broader range of future occupations' (p. 18).

HOW CAN SCHOOLS PLAY THEIR PART IN REDUCING GENDER STEREOTYPES?

Schools and Early Years settings can play their part in reducing the impact of gender stereotypes by:

- encouraging children to choose toys for themselves and motivate them to play with toys they don't normally select;

- avoiding using gendered nicknames;

- educating children and parents about the consequences of stereotypical gender roles and how to avoid guiding children towards them;

- empowering and inspiring children to be who they want to be and do what they want to do regardless of their sex or gender;

- inviting inspirational guest speakers into school to inspire children to move away from gender stereotypes;

- encourage all children to rotate classroom chores;

- empower your pupils to question the stereotypes they see around them;

- be mindful of the language we use and which behaviours we praise;

- encourage emotional literacy in all children;

- use traditional stories to discuss stereotypes with children and non-traditional stories that challenge these stereotypes to encourage curiosity and exploration;

- offer a wide range of extra-curricular activities to all children.

GENDER DIFFERENCES IN EDUCATIONAL OUTCOMES

Until the 1980s, the government was concerned about the underachievement of girls. However, since the 1990s, there has been a shift, as girls started to outperform boys in all curriculum subjects.

The data from a gov.uk (2023) report on *Key Stage 2 Attainment* shows how girls continue to outperform boys in all subjects. In 2023, 63 per cent of girls met the expected standard in reading, writing and mathematics combined, while 56 per cent of boys achieved the same, marking a seven-percentage-point gap, reduced from nine points in 2022. This reduction in the gender disparity is attributed to improved performance in reading, writing and mathematics among boys.

For many years now, girls have also outperformed boys when taking GCSEs and A-levels, although recent research suggests that the gap is narrowing. In 2023, girls outperformed boys at GCSE by 5.8 per cent (those achieving a grade 7 or above). In the 2021 A-level results, 46.4 per cent of girls achieved an A* or A grade for A-level compared to 41.7 per cent of boys. So why are girls now outperforming boys in school?

FACTORS AFFECTING GENDER DIVIDES

Gender differences in educational outcomes are influenced by various factors, such as feminist movements of their times, subcultures in schools and the impact of teachers' perceptions. This section will discuss some of the factors and explain how they affect perceptions of gender differences.

SCHOOL SUBCULTURES

The growth of *laddish* subcultures within school may also contribute to the lower scores achieved by boys (Skelton et al., 2007). Epstein (1998) studied how masculinity is constructed in schools and found that boys were more likely to be bullied for working hard and focusing in class, meaning that many of the boys studied started to reject school work in order to fit in; Jackson (2003) found that laddish behaviours may act to protect the self-worth and/or social worth of many boys, and that laddishness may be prompted by both a fear of academic failure and a fear of the feminine. Research from Houtte (2004) can also help us start to paint a picture of why girls outperform in school by arguing that boys' culture is less focused on studying than girls' culture. Teachers should work together to challenge the beliefs that lead to *anti-school* subcultures.

TEACHER INFLUENCES

Gendered subject role models may also contribute to the gender gap in school. Research from Currie et al. (2006) suggests that science is seen as a boys' subject as the majority of science teachers are male. Research from the Gender Trust (2024) also argues that male teachers dominate certain subjects such as maths, science and PE, whereas women dominate subjects such as English and languages, reinforcing gender stereotypes by acting as role models for their subjects.

THE IMPACT OF FEMINISM ON SOCIETY

Since the 1960s, there has been a shift in attitudes towards women; feminist movements have challenged the stereotypical roles of women (Ghorfati and Medini, 2015; Kaman, 2015). McRobbie's (1997) study of girls' magazines highlights a change in attitudes as magazines no longer focus on marriage and children but celebrate independent assertive women. Similarly, Sue Sharpe's (1976/1994) poignant study *Just Like A Girl* highlights the changed attitudes of girls from the 1970s to 1990s. Sharpe points out how girls in the 1970s valued love and marriage; however, by the 1990s, education and having a career that will help them to support themselves became a priority. Mitsos and Browne's (1998) research agrees, by stating how feminist movements have raised girls' expectations of themselves as well as their self-esteem.

SOCIETAL CHANGES

Changes in society, such as the 1970 Equal Pay Act, encouraged women to view their future as working women rather than as housewives (Connolly and Gregory, 2007). Additionally, the increase of divorce rates and changes to the family structure provide different role models for children.

CAREER ASPIRATIONS

Ofsted's (2011) report on *Girls' Career Aspirations* found that from a young age the girls surveyed harboured traditional stereotypes regarding gender roles in employment. These perceptions persisted throughout their schooling, despite being taught about equal opportunities and awareness of their rights to pursue any career path. This hugely affects how girls see themselves; a lack of self-confidence can affect the academic attainment of girls as they are less likely to take the risks involved to follow their dreams due to the fear of failure.

Furthermore, a study conducted by LEGO in 2024 discovered that pressure from society to be perfect is a huge risk factor in hindering girls' creativity; it found that girls as young as five had their creativity stifled as they were worried about sharing their ideas and making mistakes, preventing them from pursuing their dreams.

Harvard-trained parenting researcher and bestselling author Jennifer B Wallace says:

> When children fear failing, it can hamper their willingness to explore and think outside the box. This impacts the key skill of creative confidence – which can carry into adulthood.

> *Creative confidence is the self-assurance to generate ideas, take risks and contribute unique solutions without fear of failure. It's been found to be a cornerstone of well-being by boosting self-esteem, reducing stress, and increasing happiness, as well as a top-ranked skill for future workplaces according to the World Economic Forum. With over three quarters of girls aspiring to work in creative industries it underscores the urgent need for change.*
>
> (LEGO.com, 2024)

The findings from LEGO reveal a notable societal bias disproportionately affecting girls, as parents observe a prevalent pattern where gendered descriptors are commonly used to evaluate both males and females. Specifically, society tends to attribute terms like 'sweet', 'pretty', 'cute' and 'beautiful' predominantly to girls, while terms such as 'brave', 'cool', 'genius' and 'innovative' are more frequently associated with boys, affecting how they view themselves and their abilities.

This indicates that everyday language is actively impeding girls' ability to express themselves creatively and reach their full potential. LEGO therefore recommends that we need to alter our language to reshape the future for girls. The language we use when speaking to children should not reinforce the traditional gender roles discussed earlier. Especially when talking to girls, we need to be mindful about praising innovation and creativity over aesthetics, as more than three in five girls felt affected by society's requirement for girls to be perfect. The girls in the study reported feeling inspired and uplifted by compliments based on the principles of growth mindset, such as 'innovative', 'imaginative' and 'inspiring'.

SPORT AND EXTRA-CURRICULAR ACTIVITIES

It is also useful to pay attention to extra-curricular activities and school sport when evaluating gender differences in education as the activities that children take part in may also shape the choices they make as they progress through school.

CASE STUDY 3.1

School sport gender restrictions

In many schools, including primary, boys and girls are separated for sports. However, in a primary school in the South of England, teachers noticed that, when in the playground, boys and girls often played sports (mostly football) together. It was also noted, however, that the boys dominated the playground and had been heard asking the girls not to join in as they were 'not good enough' because they didn't have football lessons in school. The Year 4 girl pupils campaigned to have football PE lessons like the boys and the following academic year these were added to the curriculum. The majority of the girls went on to enjoy their football lessons above all sports and took part in regular local and national competitions, bringing back many trophies.

This story suggests that schools should be less restrictive with what sports their pupils can play simply based on their gender. Furthermore, the planning of the PE curriculum should be considered when choosing which sports boys and girls play in order to not discriminate. Additionally, it should be noted that segregating boys and girls for sport can lead to difficulties for children who are non-binary. Gender segregation also might change as children grow up, as there are fewer physical differences between boys and girls at age four than at age 11. This provides some food for thought when deciding whether sport should be segregated or not.

Extra-curricular clubs also play their part in reinforcing gender stereotypes. Male teachers often run clubs centred around sports, engineering and science, compared to female teachers who run clubs such as sewing, reading and craft. As these teachers act as role models for their pupils, it may not come as a surprise that the football club is predominantly filled with boys, and the sewing club with girls. Perhaps, the teachers could rotate clubs, providing children with a variety of role models to help all children attend the club of their choice, regardless of their gender.

READING FOR PLEASURE

One of the reasons for the attainment gap is that boys are less likely to read for pleasure than girls (Clark and Rumbold, 2006). Research evidence on reading for pleasure from the DfE (2012) states how there is a positive correlation between reading frequency, reading enjoyment and academic attainment (Clark, et al. 2011; Clark and Douglas, 2011). Furthermore, reading for pleasure is one of the key factors in boosting English attainment, especially with writing tasks and reading comprehension assessments. Reading also encourages children to learn more about the world, become more emotionally intelligent and improve their general knowledge.

Evidence from Clark and Douglas in 2011 found that 58 per cent of girls enjoy reading either very much or quite a lot compared to 43 per cent of boys. More recently, Clark et al. (2023) found that more girls than boys aged eight to 18 said they read daily (30.4 per cent vs 24.9 per cent), the narrower gap suggesting that the trend is starting to change. Research also suggests that boys and girls have different reading habits, as girls are more likely to read novels and stories, whereas boys are more likely to read graphic novels and comics. It is therefore vital for schools to have books that cater for the interests of all children. As boys are less likely to read for pleasure, this could help to explain the gender gap specifically in English between boys and girls.

There are numerous reading schemes that schools can adopt to encourage reading for pleasure. Accelerated Reader is a well-known platform for raising reading attainment as it adds a competitive element to reading and helps children to feel motivated to read. Once children have read a book, they complete a fun quiz based on the story and if they pass the quiz, they earn points towards reaching their target. Many schools offer prizes and incentives for children passing their targets, increasing the fun and competitive element.

> ## REFLECTION 3.3
>
> What approaches can your school consider to overcome the gender divide? Think about the role encouraging reading for pleasure can play in tackling gender disparity. Here are some ideas to start you off:
>
> - inviting inspiring authors of all genders into school;
>
> - providing a wide selection of books for children to choose from;
>
> - investing in a reading scheme that works for the children in that setting and sticking with it to create routine;
>
> - introducing reading challenges and events to inspire children to enjoy reading;
>
> - celebrating book-related events, such as Book Week, World Book Day and Drop Everything and Read Day.

SO, WHAT IS CHANGING?

Although recent research suggests that the gender attainment gap is still very much apparent, new statistics suggest that boys are catching up, especially in science, technology, engineering and maths (STEM)-related subjects. In mathematics, boys have traditionally outperformed girls at A-level, though that may be reversing. Of the GCSEs taken by girls 25.3 per cent were graded 7 or above in 2023 (equivalent to A and A*), similar to the 25.1 per cent seen before the Covid-19 pandemic. However, 19.5 per cent of boys' entries received a top grade this year – 0.9 points higher than in 2019. The gender gap reduced to 5.8 percentage points – its lowest level since 2016 (Goodier, 2023).

GIRLS IN SCIENCE, TECHNOLOGY, ENGINEERING AND MATHS (STEM)

Girls are often encouraged to consider taking STEM subjects across all key stages in school; however, it is unclear whether this has been successful or not in reducing gender disparity. In September 2020, T-levels (two-year technical courses) were introduced, allowing children to study subjects such as construction, engineering and manufacturing. The government aimed to challenge gender stereotypes by using T-Level ambassadors to 'showcase a wide range of voices' from those already studying the qualifications, including girls taking STEM-related subjects. The government funded the Stimulating Physics Network, which was designed to encourage girls to choose physics for A-level. Additionally, the government invested to create the National Centre for Computing Education with the aim of improving computing education and to encourage girls to choose computer science for their GCSEs and A-levels. The website Women in Science Day also promotes a love of science among girls, encouraging them to pursue these interests inside and outside school.

CASE STUDY 3.2

Boys' attainment

In 1999, Cawdell conducted a study at a school in Guildford which was struggling with raising boys' attainment. The case study found that boys responded better and achieved more when they were set small, manageable targets by their teachers, rather than simply being told to 'work harder'. It helped the boys to see their own progress more quickly which provided them with motivation. The study concluded that positive praise was a huge factor in improving boys' academic attainment, along with the creation of warm, positive relationships with staff. When the boys felt supported to achieve well, they were more motivated and worked harder.

Although this case study is dated the ideas suggested above are widely used by teachers today; the findings of this case have contributed significantly to shaping teachers' ideas about how to help boys achieve well in the classroom. It demonstrates how boys' attainment can be improved by making some tweaks to the classroom environment.

REFLECTION 3.4

One way of raising boys' attainment is by focusing on their literacy skills, through encouraging boys to engage with reading and help them to discover a love of creative writing. Make a list of books that might encourage boys to read in your classroom.

You can even engage your pupils in a class audit and empower them in the process.

It is important to note that schools should focus their attention where they fall short academically. For example, if boys are underachieving in English, improving literacy should be the focus. In order to raise boys' attainment, the laddish and anti-school subcultures often formed by boys in school perhaps need to be challenged (Jackson, 2003). These subcultures hold values that oppose those of the education system; however, numerous studies prove that it is possible to change the attitudes of these subcultures by reframing their ideas about education. As mentioned in the previous section of this chapter, it is possible to improve boys' attitudes to learning by creating positive interactions between pupils and teachers, using positive praise to promote success and through carefully planned mentoring sessions.

THE IMPORTANCE OF REDUCING GENDER BIAS

This section highlights the importance of reducing gender differences in schools as experiences in education have a long-term impact on life chances, including education and career opportunities.

IMPACT ON HIGHER EDUCATION

In 2016, UCAS revealed that women were 35 per cent more likely to go university than men. There is no surprise here considering the statistics set out in this chapter, highlighting how girls outperform boys at every stage of education. The Green Paper *Fulfilling Our Potential* (BIS, 2016) was set out by the government in 2016 with the aim of reducing the gender gap for university applicants. However, UCAS's Chief Executive Mary Curnock Cook argued that although these schemes have been focusing on boys, attempts are futile if boys are still too far behind by the time they leave secondary school.

Although women are more likely to attend university than men, they are much less likely to choose STEM degrees, suggesting that the gender stereotypes embedded during school still have a significant impact on children by the time they reach university age. It is therefore imperative that teachers challenge stereotypes in schools and make use of initiatives to reduce gender stereotypes in order to narrow the gender gap at university.

CAREERS

The importance of reducing the gender gap in education for the benefit of both boys and girls alike cannot be underrated, as children carry their qualifications, but also the gender stereotypes and views about themselves with them throughout their lives.

The US Bureau of Labour statistics (2022) revealed that women made up just over 58 per cent of the workforce; 6.5 per cent of them worked in male-dominated occupations. Among men, 5.4 per cent worked in female-dominated occupations. These figures suggest that gender stereotypes still very much remain, with 82 per cent of participants believing that certain jobs are associated with a specific gender.

The University of Plymouth (n.d.) highlights that 'men training to become nurses has plateaued for decades at between 8–11% [sic]' and HEPI reports that only 29 per cent of modern languages students are men (Bowler, 2020). Meanwhile, the Gender Action Portal (https://gap.hks.harvard.edu/) reminds us how men are still significantly more likely to graduate with STEM degrees, which often lead to higher-earning careers, suggesting that the effects of gender stereotypes can prevent women from accessing top jobs in certain fields and prevent men from entering others. Ultimately, the beliefs that children internalise about themselves due to the presentation of gender stereotypes from an early age can play a significant role in shaping that child's life, affecting their choice of school subjects, university and, therefore, also career choices. This presents questions about whether these embedded ideas can be changed and undone and what schools and society can do to help.

HOW CAN SCHOOLS HELP TO REDUCE GENDER DIFFERENCES?

In summary, schools can help reduce gender differences by being aware of them, thinking outside the box and challenging longstanding assumptions about gender roles.

One way to do this is by developing a love for reading, which can be encouraged by inviting inspirational authors into school, following robust reading schemes and introducing fun incentives. It would also be beneficial to challenge the attitudes of laddish male anti-school subcultures by avoiding reinforcing gender stereotypes through teacher role models. Furthermore, making use of 'girls in STEM' initiatives and encouraging challenge of gender stereotypes would go a long way in reducing gender differences. Teachers should make an effort to present both genders equally in lessons and reduce the segregation of boys and girls where possible. Offering a wide range of extra-curricular activities for all children would also expose them to a wide variety of job prospects and career options from an early age, thereby helping to reduce the potential barriers caused by deep-rooted prejudices linked with gender differences.

GENDER IS CHANGING

This chapter cannot be concluded without acknowledging that our understanding of gender is changing. The concept of what 'gender' means and how we explore it is constantly evolving which is both exciting and challenging. By reconsidering gender roles, such as by encouraging boys to enjoy subjects traditionally associated with girls and vice versa, as well as by accommodating children's self-expression and understanding of themselves, schools can create an environment for young people to thrive and be curious about what their own values and interests are, rather than those imposed by traditional society.

■■ CHAPTER SUMMARY ■■■■■■■■■■■■■■■■■■■■■■■■■■■■

Within this chapter we have considered:

- possible explanations for why there is gender bias and assumptions are made in schools;

- ways in which we can reduce gender differences in school that affect educational outcomes;

- how the socialisation of children can affect their views about themselves and about gender.

FURTHER READING

Challenging Gender Stereotypes in Education by Karen Jones (2020)

This book supports its readers to understand, recognise and challenge gender stereotypes in schools and offers practical guidance and strategies to combat these.

Gender Equality in Primary Schools: A Guide for Teachers by Helen Griffin (2018)

This book supports educators to challenge gender stereotypes and provides advice on how to promote gender equality and respect in all areas of school life.

Not Only Pink and Blue

www.notonlypinkandblue.com/

This website offers up-to-date practical advice to help parents and educators to reduce gender differences and remove barriers that gender discrimination creates to produce future generations of equal children.

Why We Need More Men to Become Nurses. University of Plymouth (n.d.)

www.plymouth.ac.uk/schools/school-of-nursing-and-midwifery/men-in-nursing

This article aims to bust the myth about nursing being a 'female' career as it campaigns for more men to smash stereotypes and apply for a nursing degree.

4

EXCLUSION (DISABILITY)

GEORGIA VENESS AND ELIZABETH BLAKEMAN

THIS CHAPTER

The chapter will provide opportunities for readers to reflect upon:

- why, based on current statistics, it is likely teacher trainees or class teachers will be responsible for children with disabilities in the classroom
- what some of the different conditions are that a child may have which could lead to them being identified for disability support
- what some inclusive practices that can support children with disabilities are
- how confident they would be in supporting children with disabilities.

DEFINITIONS

To begin this chapter, we highlight some of the key terms and definitions that you may come across:

- *Disability*: a physical or mental impairment that has a *substantial* and *long-term* negative effect on one's ability to do normal daily activities.

INTRODUCTION

In the bustling halls and classrooms of our schools, the echoes of laughter and the hum of learning fills the air. Yet, amid the hubbub of school life, a struggle exists that often goes unnoticed: the experience of exclusion faced by children with disabilities. This chapter will delve into the intricate web of challenges and complexities that surround the intersection of disability and schooling, shedding light on the profound impact it has on the lives of children living with disabilities.

This chapter acknowledges the fundamental truth that every child deserves a nurturing and inclusive educational environment, where their unique abilities and perspectives are celebrated and valued. However, for many children with disabilities, the reality falls far short of this ideal. Instead of feeling embraced by their peers and educators, they often find themselves on the periphery of school life, grappling with feelings of isolation.

In this chapter, we will also examine how societal attitudes, institutional barriers and stakeholder relationships intersect to create learning environments for children with disabilities. The barriers faced by children with disabilities are disruptive to their education, such as limited access to parts of their school, limited funding for appropriate resources and also a lack of understanding from their teachers and peers.

This chapter will also explore the emotional toll that exclusion can take on children with disabilities, as they navigate school life, highlighting the ways in which exclusion shapes their sense of self-worth, belonging and personal and communal identities. We will spotlight innovative intervention ideas and practical applications that will help to create inclusive school communities, where every child is empowered and encouraged to thrive.

WHAT IS DISABILITY EXCLUSION?

The Equality Act (2010) states that schools must not discriminate against or exclude a pupil due to them having a disability. However, not discriminating against a child for having a disability is not enough; schools and teachers must take positive and proactive steps to enable disabled pupils to access and participate in the same curriculum activities as other pupils, helping them to access all aspects of the education they are entitled to. Schools must work hard to become inclusive and remove barriers that may prevent a disabled child from receiving the same educational opportunities (or as close as possible) as other pupils, such as by providing access arrangements to enter the school, provisions for school trips and specialised resources where necessary (IPSEA, 2024). Additionally, disabled children have the right to a tailored education plan, often outlined in an education, health and care plan (EHCP), which identifies their specific needs and outlines the support they require to thrive academically and socially.

Kearney (2008) argues that disability exclusion can happen when disabled children are devalued in school, but also when they face a barrier or obstacle to receiving the education they deserve, as a valued member of the school. This can happen when disabled children have restricted access to all the necessary ingredients required to receive a full education, such as, extra-curricular experiences and school trips, school resources, friendships, school rewards and the amount of teacher time they require. Booth and Ainscow (1998) further this definition, by stating that exclusion is the process of decreasing the participation from a particular group of pupils from a school's curriculum and culture.

4 Exclusion

From reviewing the relevant literature in this field, it is clear that most research surrounding exclusion focuses on the disciplinary process of removing a child from school and very little literature focuses on exclusion within schools. It must also be noted that the small amount of literature that does focus on exclusion within school is quite dated, suggesting that there is a gap in the research here which needs to be explored further to understand what the picture actually looks like in school and what can be done to reduce this type of exclusion.

Davis and Watson (2001) argue that, previously, not enough has been done to reduce disability exclusion in schools, by stating that this type of exclusion will not be eliminated until teachers and adults who work with children put themselves into the child's shoes and really try to understand the barriers to education that disabled children can face. Furthermore, they argue that children should be more involved with amending policies related to inclusive education and have their voices heard when it comes to adjusting policies and practices that will affect those children and the experience they have of education.

The book *Extraordinary Bodies* (Thomson, 2017) furthers the idea that, in order to help disabled children live in a world that is not yet set up well enough for disabled people, adults who work with disabled children must learn how to be disabled and how to achieve well-being and competence while living with a disability. The book suggests that this is the only way that disabled people can feel the shift from being isolated to becoming part of a community that celebrates them for who they are, rather than trying to make them become non-disabled.

WHY DISABLED PUPILS MIGHT FEEL EXCLUDED

Disabled children may feel excluded from school for a multitude of reasons, stemming primarily from societal misconceptions, lack of accessibility and inadequate support systems. Inaccessible physical environments can pose significant barriers to their participation in school life, whether it's navigating stairs without ramps or encountering inaccessible bathrooms. Moreover, a lack of understanding and empathy from peers can exacerbate feelings of isolation and often results in bullying behaviours towards those disabled pupils for being 'different'. Educational materials and teaching methods might not cater to their diverse needs, leading to frustration and disengagement. Additionally, the absence of inclusive policies and practices within schools can further perpetuate a sense of exclusion, denying these children the opportunity to fully participate in academic and social activities. As a result, disabled children may experience a profound sense of alienation, hindering their overall well-being and educational development, highlighting that more needs to be done to improve the educational journeys for these children.

THE PICTURE IN THE UK

In the UK, there is a significant number of children living with disabilities who are actively enrolled in schools. According to recent statistics from Long et al. (2023), in January 2022, there were around 1.5 million pupils with identified SEN (around 17 per cent of pupils in England), with approximately 3 per cent having EHCPs outlining their specific needs and required support. The majority of these pupils attend mainstream schools. In January 2022, there were 1,022 state-funded special schools in England, with around 142,000 pupils recorded as attending them. These figures reflect a diverse range of disabilities, including but not limited to physical impairments, sensory disabilities, learning difficulties and mental health conditions. Additionally, there has been a noticeable increase in the enrolment of disabled children in mainstream schools since the 2010 Equality Act (DfE, 2010), reflecting a broader societal shift towards inclusive education and meaning that it is likely that teacher trainees and class teachers will be responsible for children with disabilities in the classroom, providing challenges that will be discussed later in the chapter. Disparities in educational attainment and access to support services persist among disabled children, highlighting the ongoing need for greater awareness, resources and inclusive practices within schools.

In the pursuit of inclusion in UK schools, dilemmas and tensions often arise concerning the practice of 'labelling' disabled children. While labels such as *disabled* or *special educational needs* can facilitate access to necessary support and resources, they also carry the risk of stigmatisation and low expectations. The act of labelling can sometimes lead to the perception of disabled children as fundamentally different or deficient, potentially impacting their self-esteem and social integration within the school community. Furthermore, there is a tension between the desire to provide personalised support through individual plans like EHCPs and the risk of inadvertently segregating disabled children from their peers. Balancing the need for targeted interventions with the goal of fostering inclusive environments where all students are valued for their unique abilities presents a significant challenge for educators and policy-makers.

A SHIFT TOWARDS MAINSTREAM SCHOOL INCLUSION

In the UK, there has been a notable shift towards inclusive education, with a focus on integrating disabled children into mainstream schools rather than segregating them in special schools. This movement is driven by the recognition of the rights of all children to access quality education in an inclusive environment, as enshrined in legislation such as the Equality Act 2010 and the United Nations Convention on the Rights of Persons with Disabilities (UNCRPD). Under these laws, schools are required to make reasonable adjustments to ensure disabled children can access education without discrimination (gov. uk, n.d.). Inclusive education promotes diversity, equity and social cohesion by fostering opportunities for disabled and non-disabled children to learn together, promoting understanding, empathy and respect for differences. Moreover, Shaw (2017) suggests that inclusive education can lead to better academic and social outcomes for disabled children as it provides access to a wider range of resources, experiences and peer interactions and provides aspirations for disabled children. While challenges remain in ensuring adequate support and accommodations within mainstream schools, the shift towards inclusion reflects a commitment to creating a more equitable and inclusive education system that recognises and celebrates the diversity of all learners.

PHYSICAL DISABILITIES

Various physical disabilities can significantly impact a child's education by presenting unique challenges that may hinder their ability to fully participate in academic and social activities that make up school life. For instance, mobility impairments such as paralysis or muscular dystrophy can affect a child's access to the physical environment, making it difficult to navigate school buildings or participate in physical education lessons. Sensory impairments like blindness or deafness can impede communication and comprehension, requiring specialised instructional methods and assistive technologies. Chronic health conditions such as asthma or epilepsy may result in frequent absences or interruptions to learning. Additionally, conditions like cerebral palsy can affect fine motor skills, making tasks like writing or using classroom materials challenging. Overall, these diverse physical disabilities may necessitate individualised accommodations, support and accessibility modifications to ensure that all children have equal opportunities to learn and succeed in school.

Physical disabilities come in many forms, but some of the main examples from the Better Health Channel (www.betterhealth.vic.gov.au/health/servicesandsupport/physical-disabilities) include:

- amputations and loss of limbs

- arthritis

- birth defects

- cerebral palsy

- cystic fibrosis

- epilepsy

- neural tube defects

- spinal cord injuries

- maintaining a healthy weight

4 Exclusion

- blindness

- deafness.

Children with these disabilities will all experience life differently, but they can have similar experiences of exclusion in school. Let's consider some of these disabilities in the context of the classroom.

CASE STUDY 4.1

Deafness and silence

Lottie is a nine-year-old deaf girl who attends school in the South of England. Since this disability is not explicitly visible, and there is a lack of education around deafness, some of her teachers and peers mistakenly believed that Lottie could not perceive sound. In reality, just 12 per cent of deaf children in the UK are profoundly deaf (NDCS, n.d.b); this means that sounds below 95dB cannot be heard (see www.sense.org.uk/information-and-advice/conditions/deafness-and-hearing-loss/). Therefore, many deaf children, including Lottie, have some degree of residual hearing and can detect various sounds, especially with hearing devices. Some severely deaf children may perceive loud noises, specific pitches, or environmental sounds, which can be essential in their learning and daily interactions.

When Lottie was learning to read, her teachers thought that systematic synthetic phonics (SSP) was the best method for teaching phonics to the whole class. They thought that since Lottie was wearing hearing aids, she could hear well enough to benefit from SSP. However, Lottie's hearing aids did not restore normal hearing; they only amplified sound, making it difficult for her to distinguish between different phonetic sounds, a critical component of SSP.

Instead, *cued speech* was found to be much more effective for Lottie, as this technique uses hand shapes and placements along with mouth movements to represent sounds visually. It was particularly challenging for Lottie to distinguish the difference in sound between 'p', 'm' and 'b' as each sound uses the same lip pattern (Ridgway, 2016). Cued speech bridges the gap between spoken language and its written form; this technique offers the visual cues that SSP lacks. Moreover, incorporating visual aids and multimodal teaching strategies, such as visual phonics and interactive whiteboards, significantly enhanced the learning experience for Lottie. Music is also a good strategy to engage children like Lottie in school. Deaf children can learn to understand music, not just through auditory means, but also by feeling vibrations (Darrow, 2006). They can sense the rhythm and beat of music through vibrations, a powerful way to engage with and enjoy musical activities. Simple adjustments can be made to music tuition, such as considering the environment and using soft furnishings that do not have background noise (NDCS, n.d.a).

4 Exclusion

It is clear from this case study that teachers need to be aware of how they can improve access to the curriculum for all disabled children in their classrooms. Schools should focus some CPD and inset training on supporting disabled children.

MENTAL DISABILITIES

Mental disabilities can profoundly impact a child's education by influencing their cognitive, emotional and behavioural functioning in many ways. Conditions such as autism spectrum disorder (ASD) can affect social interactions, communication skills and sensory processing, making it challenging to engage effectively in classroom activities. Attention-deficit/hyperactivity disorder (ADHD) can lead to difficulties in focusing, organising tasks and regulating impulses, affecting academic performance and classroom behaviour. Let's consider how ADHD can often be misunderstood as poor behaviour.

CASE STUDY 4.2

ADHD or poor behaviour?

Jacob is an 11-year-old boy with ADHD who attends school in the North West of England. He loves being creative in lessons and answering questions and is always keen to please his teachers. Jacob, however, also struggles with focusing in lessons, sitting still and staying on task, which is often difficult for his teachers to manage and is disruptive for the learning in the classroom. Many of Jacob's teachers label him as 'naughty' and he often gets sanctioned for his behaviour, especially when he shouts out in lessons and is caught running in the corridor. Jacob often becomes frustrated and confused by the sanctions he receives as he finds it very difficult to control his outbursts of energy and impulsive actions.

ADHD is estimated to affect about 2–5 per cent (around 1 in 30) pupils at school; the *core symptoms* are usually present before the child is 12 years old and can persist throughout their school life. Boys are often reported as exhibiting overactive features and as a result can be perceived as more difficult to manage.

Teachers need to understand how to help children with ADHD manage their symptoms to optimise their learning. Some strategies that can be helpful in a classroom setting are:

- allowing children with ADHD to have reasonable and regular movement breaks, or allowing them to work standing up rather than being stuck at a desk can help these children to refocus and stay on task;

- providing opportunities for children with ADHD to learn creatively through physically making or exploring topics through play rather than using traditional teaching methods can also help to engage these pupils;

56

- using these strategy examples can help teachers to reframe their preconceived notions of how to manage children with ADHD.

> **REFLECTION 4.1**
>
> How do you think these strategies could be used to support children with other mental disabilities in the classroom?
>
> Can you think of some practical ways you might employ these strategies in your practice?

Learning disabilities such as dyslexia or dyscalculia can impede reading, writing, or mathematical abilities, requiring specialised instructional strategies and interventions. Mental health disorders like anxiety or depression can interfere with concentration, motivation and overall well-being, impacting attendance and participation in school. These various mental disabilities require comprehensive assessment, intervention and support services to address their specific needs and enable optimal educational outcomes for children. Some of these disabilities are classed as SEN, if children have a learning problem or disability that makes it more difficult for them to learn than most children their age (gov.uk, n.d.). Chapter 5 will discuss SEN at length: the challenges teachers and pupils face in the classroom; and what teachers can do to understand and support their SEN pupils.

DISABILITY VS SEN?

It is important to note that children with SEN may not always have a disability, just as some disabled children may not require special educational support. However, Keil et al. (2006) argue that there is considerable overlap between these two groups.

On the one hand, disabilities refer to impairments – whether physical, cognitive, sensory, or emotional – that significantly limit an individual's functioning in various aspects of life, including learning. These impairments can range from mobility limitations to intellectual disabilities or sensory impairments. On the other hand, SEN encompass a broader spectrum of requirements that may arise from disabilities, but also include other factors such as learning difficulties, behavioural challenges, or emotional issues that require additional support to access education effectively. SEN can affect children without necessarily being classified as disabilities, and they may require specialised interventions and teaching methods tailored to their individual needs. In essence, while disabilities denote specific impairments, SEN encompass a wider range of challenges that may impact a child's learning and development.

VISIBILITY

Disability visibility refers to the inclusion and portrayal of people with disabilities in various aspects of society, including media, education, employment and public spaces.

It emphasises the importance of recognising and representing the diverse experiences and contributions of individuals with disabilities, ensuring their voices are heard and their needs are addressed. Effective representation challenges stereotypes, promotes understanding and advocates for equal opportunities, creating a more inclusive and equitable society where everyone, regardless of ability, can participate fully and authentically.

DISABILITY VISIBILITY IN LITERATURE

Disabled children need to feel understood and represented in literature and will often seek characters in the books they read who reflect their own experiences, yet disabilities are not consistently depicted accurately or positively in children's literature. It's crucial to positively display disabilities in children's books to help disabled children feel seen and celebrated, not ashamed of their disability. Furthermore, since all children will encounter disabilities in various aspects of life, whether firsthand, within their families, or at school among their peers, it's essential for children to encounter literature where disabilities are accepted, celebrated and portrayed in a positive light to promote a better understanding. Cheyne (2019) argues that disability representation in literature is essential to encourage the reader to reflect upon what they understand about disability, and potentially to rethink it and remove any negative connotations they may have held about disability.

Schnoover (2021) suggests some useful books that promote advocacy and raise awareness about physical and mental disabilities in a manner that is positive and accessible to children. They refrain from depicting disabilities as problems to be solved, but instead foster an appreciation for the diverse lives led by the characters.

It is important to note here that teachers should search for literature that represents specific disabilities of children in their class to help them feel represented in the school community, but also to help their peers understand what life is like for them living with their disability. Representation in literature also shapes children's perceptions about what the world is like, so teaching using such literature will help children to understand the diversity of the world.

Past trends in inclusion literature suggest that advancements towards diversity are being made. A review of 59 children's books conducted by Ayala in 1999, with the aim of assessing both their literary merit and their reflection of the educational and demographic patterns of society, found a notable increase in the overall quantity of published books and a broader spectrum of disabilities depicted in recent works.

However, the study found several shortcomings: minimal representation of ethnically diverse characters, scarcity of books in languages other than English and a lack of emphasis on specific cultural traditions and differences. Given the rich cultural and linguistic diversity within our school systems, the scarcity of children's literature showcasing multiethnic characters with disabilities highlights a significant disparity between literature and real life.

Beckett et al.'s (2010) study highlights that although there has been progress in the amount of available representative literature there is still evidence of disabled people being discriminated against in children's literature; they go on to argue that authors need specific training in disability awareness to help make literature more representative to celebrate all different bodies and also remind people that disability is normal in society and something that should be openly represented. Furthermore, findings from this study suggest that teachers should be directed to high-quality examples of inclusion literature to help all children feel seen and represented. Schnoover (2021) has more recently reviewed inclusion literature and found that disabilities are often not portrayed accurately or positively, suggesting that although disabilities may be depicted more in literature, it is still not being done correctly.

Sigurjónsdóttir (2015) argues that, traditionally, disabilities have not been positively depicted by society and that some of the stigma around disability is due to society not having a great enough understanding of different disabilities. Furthermore, this research argues that historical folk tales and stories have contributed to these negative connotations. In the story of Heidi, for instance, Clara regains her ability to walk after Peter pushes her wheelchair off a rock. Over a century later, in an Icelandic children's tale, a blind girl miraculously regains her sight after being struck on the head with a wooden plank by a burglar. In both narratives, violence is portrayed as the means to cure a disability.

Many advancements have been made in terms of how disability is represented in literature today due to the development of new understandings and government policies and legislation; however, Sigurjónsdóttir (2015) still found that new representative literature is less widely read than traditional tales that are passed between generations, supporting the view from Beckett et al. (2010) that teachers and also parents need to be directed towards examples of inclusive literature to help children understand the diversity of society and also help disabled children feel represented.

LEARNING RESOURCE 4.1

Schnoover (2021) suggests some useful books that promote advocacy and raise awareness about physical and mental disabilities in a manner that is positive and accessible to children. They refrain from depicting disabilities as problems to be solved, but instead foster an appreciation for the diverse lives led by the characters.

The books Schnoover recommends include:

- *Why Does Izzy Cover Her Ears?* by Jennifer Veenendall

- *Moses Goes to a Concert* by Isaac Millman

- *The Seeing Stick* by Jane Yolen

- *Red: A Crayon's Story* by Michael Hall

- *We'll Paint the Octopus Red* by Stephanie Stuve-Bodeen.

DISABILITY VISIBILITY IN TEACHING RESOURCES

In addition to disabled children needing to be represented in literature, they also need to be represented in teaching resources to feel part of the school community. This includes pictures of children with different disabilities displayed in textbooks and shown during teaching PowerPoints in all subjects. After reviewing popular websites with access to teaching resources such as Twinkl and Classroom Secrets, it is clear that some progress has been made to represent disabled children throughout their visual teaching tools; however, not enough is being done. When examples have been found that do represent disabled children, they depict the child in a wheelchair the majority of the time, rather than representing children with a whole range of different disabilities. This is something for teachers to be aware of when teaching disabled children, as teachers should strive to find or make teaching resources that represent a pupil's particular disability, rather than their resources always depicting more able-bodied children.

REFLECTION 4.2

Look at the teaching resources you are currently using.

Do you feel like they are representative enough of all children, including those with disabilities?

Are there resources you could replace with more diverse and inclusive versions?

REDUCING DISABILITY EXCLUSION

Schools must take a multifaceted approach in order to promote inclusion and provide the best support for their disabled pupils. Kearney (2011) argues that one key aspect of support involves early identification and intervention through comprehensive assessment processes to identify children's specific needs and strengths. This is often facilitated through collaboration between teachers, parents and specialist professionals. Additionally, implementing inclusive teaching strategies that cater to diverse learning styles and abilities ensures that all students can actively participate and engage in the learning process. Providing access to assistive technologies, adapted resources and auxiliary aids further enhances accessibility and removes barriers to learning. Furthermore, fostering a supportive and inclusive school culture that celebrates diversity, raises awareness and promotes empathy helps create a welcoming environment where children with disabilities feel valued, respected and empowered to reach their full potential. Collaborative initiatives between schools, local authorities and community organisations also play a crucial role in coordinating resources and support services to meet the diverse needs of children with disabilities. Schools should work closely with the parents and families of disabled children to ensure the best possible learning environment at home and in school. Regular communication should take place in terms of reviewing progress, providing support and suggesting next steps for success. Teachers should also strive to use teaching resources and literature that represents disabled children to help them feel celebrated and seen among the school community.

gov.uk (n.d.) suggests the following ideas as reasonable adjustments that schools should make in order to accommodate their pupils with physical and mental disabilities; however, it is not comprehensive enough to advise or support teachers:

- a pupil with a visual impairment sits at the back of the class to accommodate their field of vision;

- school uniform is adapted for a pupil who has an allergy to synthetic material or severe eczema;

- a healthy snacks policy is adjusted for a pupil with diabetes who needs a high-calorie snack at breaktime;

- special communication systems like traffic light cards are put in place for a pupil who needs extra time to complete a task;

- a pupil with dyslexia who struggles to write on white paper uses different coloured paper;

- a short-term reduced timetable is agreed for a pupil with ASD or ADHD who finds classroom environments intimidating, in order to build their confidence back up to full-time attendance;

- amendments to access arrangements to help a physically disabled child access a school space.

TEACHER EXPERIENCES WORKING WITH DISABLED CHILDREN

Teachers may encounter challenges in adequately supporting disabled children due to various factors within the education system. Limited resources and training in inclusive education can leave teachers ill-equipped to address the diverse needs of disabled pupils effectively. The diversity of disabilities, ranging from physical impairments to learning difficulties, can present a daunting task for teachers seeking to provide tailored support. Additionally, Cook and Ogden (2022) argue that high teacher-to-student ratios and heavy workloads may hinder the ability to give individualised attention and support. Furthermore, societal stigmas and misconceptions surrounding disability can influence teachers' attitudes and perceptions, leading to unintentional biases or lowered expectations for disabled students. Without sufficient support structures and professional development opportunities, teachers may struggle to create truly inclusive learning environments where all pupils can thrive.

4 Exclusion

Teachers may also have concerns about inadvertently causing harm or exacerbating challenges for pupils with disabilities, contributing to teacher apprehension. Moreover, the pressure to meet academic standards and manage classroom dynamics within limited time frames can further reduce a teacher's confidence when it comes to catering to the needs of pupils with disabilities. Robinson (2017) suggests that addressing these challenges requires ongoing professional development, access to resources and support networks and a shift towards a more inclusive and collaborative approach to education.

Teacher confidence in effectively teaching disabled children also plays a role in the support these children receive. Anecdotal evidence from a local primary school suggests that teachers have varied levels of confidence when it comes to teaching children with disabilities, due to the knowledge they may have of different disabilities and experiences they may have had personally, among their family or through their local communities. As discussed in this chapter, children may have physical or mental disabilities; there is a plethora of different disabilities that a child could have, meaning that teachers have a lot to learn when it comes to supporting disabled children.

REFLECTION 4.3

Can you list some things that you, as a school, do to support your disabled pupils?

Can you list some things you do in your personal practice to support disabled pupils?

Can you list some further things you could do?

EVIDENCE OF GOOD PRACTICE

A primary school in England has found that when teachers dedicate copious amounts of time to understand a child's disability and also their experiences of living with it, it produces positive results for both teachers and pupils alike. This may have ramifications for teachers' existing workloads.

Sometimes, teachers may have more knowledge about certain disabilities than others and teachers should regularly work with the school's special educational needs coordinator (SENCO) and other specialists to gain a better understanding of certain disabilities. This may be difficult for teachers who do not have access to certain specialists, or who have large class sizes, or multiple disabled children in their class. This is why creating such inclusive spaces within schools is the responsibility of not just the class teacher, but also the senior management team.

Additionally, more work needs to be done to better prepare student teachers through university teaching courses and also through in-school CPD to help teachers support the disabled children they work with. Teaching assistants (TAs) are also integral to the education of pupils with disabilities, often providing specialised support on a one-on-one basis without direct teacher oversight. Despite this, there nowadays is a scarcity of training programmes tailored to helping adults support disabled children in the classroom. This poses a huge problem for the inclusion and progression of disabled pupils, as not having the necessary knowledge to support their practice, non-specialist TAs can be hindered in their ability to provide effective support to disabled pupils, often preventing their academic progress.

REFLECTION 4.4

Think about whether you currently feel like you have enough knowledge and resources to support your disabled pupils.

If more work needs to be done, consider which routes you might take to achieve this.

CONCLUSION

This chapter has outlined the picture in the UK for children with disabilities attending school and has discussed some of the challenges faced by educators due to a lack of training, lack of funding and lack of support to effectively teach disabled children. The move towards inclusion was aimed to help disabled children feel integrated and valued, but this leads to questions of whether they are actually in a better position in mainstream schools, with teachers lacking in knowledge and confidence. This chapter has highlighted that with the shift towards inclusion, more needs to be done through university courses and CPD to equip teachers with the knowledge and skills needed to successfully support disabled children to ensure that they receive the education they are entitled to.

CHAPTER SUMMARY

Within this chapter we have considered:

- that SEN and disability are not synonymous; we have explored differences between SEN and disability;

- the current context in terms of number of children living with disabilities in UK schools;

- some key policy developments relating to disabilities;

- some dilemmas and tensions relating to inclusion and labelling;

- some best practice and initiatives to support children with disabilities.

FURTHER READING AND RESOURCES

Extraordinary Bodies by Rosemarie Garland Thomson (updated version published in 2017)

This book is a cornerstone text for disability studies; it has laid the foundations for valuing disability culture and introduced an inclusive, innovative approach to studying social marginalisation.

Disability Visibility by Alice Wong (2020)

This book contains a collection of modern first-person stories, helping us all to step into the shoes of those living with disabilities.

The Inclusive Classroom by Daniel Sobel and Sara Alston (2021)

This book is an outstanding guide to evolving inclusion strategies and fostering a culture where every child can thrive in your classroom.

5
CHALLENGING ABLEISM AND NEURONORMATIVITY

AMY BOYD

THIS CHAPTER

The chapter will provide opportunities for readers to reflect upon:

- the different conditions a child may have which could lead to them being identified for SEN support
- the tensions surrounding SEN, and how parents' attitudes may vary over their child being identified as SEN
- inclusive practices that can support children with SEN
- your responsibility and confidence in supporting children with SEN.

DEFINITIONS

To begin this chapter, we highlight some of the key terms and definitions that you may come across:

- *Ableism*: this is the discrimination of and social prejudice against people with disabilities based on the belief that typical abilities are superior. Ableism is rooted in the assumption that disabled people require 'fixing' and defines people by their disability. Ableism in the primary classroom is often overlooked or underrepresented in developing awareness about discrimination and social justice in primary-aged pupils. This is particularly true for neurological disorders, which are not always immediately visible or easy to understand.

- *Neuronormativity*: this is a set of norms, standards and expectations reinforced throughout society which normalises a particular way of functioning including thinking, feeling, communicating and behaving. This way of functioning is seen as the superior and often correct way.

INTRODUCTION

Ableism and neuronormativity are two hot issues within educational discourse today. There has been an increase in concern among policy-makers, teachers, school leaders, parents and communities regarding children with SEND becoming excluded as a direct result of these issues. SEND is a popular acronym used in the education system, standing for *special educational needs and disabilities*. As disability has been previously discussed in Chapter 4, we will just be examining the SEN side of education here, diving into the big issues surrounding children with SEN in schools and attempting to consolidate the separation of SEN and disability, which is often used synonymously under the umbrella term 'SEND'. We will also be addressing the current context of SEN in schools through the recent school statistics and data, government documentation and policies. In a nutshell, this chapter will consider what inclusion of SEN children means in school settings, for you as a teacher, and suggest ways to implement this in your classroom to make learning more inclusive and accessible for all learners.

CHALLENGING ABLEISM AND NEURONORMATIVITY

Ableism results in the devaluation of disabled and neurodivergent people in favour of those deemed as able, resulting in discrimination. The Equality Act (DfE, 2010) states that schools must not discriminate against a pupil because of their disability or additional needs, but mainstream classrooms are usually equipped for standard learning with little scope of additional support or provision for children with learning difficulties. Ableism is one of the less prevalent dynamics of privilege, which should be considered more widely in school settings. School buildings and education policies both tend to be designed by 'privileged' and mainly non-disabled professionals who often may, for example, miss considerations of alternative entrances or pathways which may contain steps. Even lack of consideration of flexible options for uniforms to accommodate some children who may have sensitivities to certain textiles may be a discriminatory act.

SHOULD WE BE PROMOTING NEURODIVERSITY, RATHER THAN NEURONORMATIVITY?

In our society, the concept of *normal* tends to be deeply engrained, influencing how we perceive the world around us. This concept is an inadvertent action, which is normalised by society. It has previously been suggested that neuronormativity disadvantages everyone, not just neurodivergent individuals. Examples of promoting neuronormativity include:

- expecting individuals to learn and gain knowledge by reading or writing;

- expecting everyone to communicate through spoken language;

- expecting children to continue working with noise in the background;

- expecting all children to have similar emotions about 'fun' activities.

When we promote neuronormativity in schools, we marginalise and stigmatise children who fall outside the neurotypical spectrum. This includes children with autism, ADHD and many other neurological differences. Society's expectations are typically structured to accommodate only neurotypical behaviour, leaving others at a disadvantage. This leads to increased levels of difficulty for neurodiverse children during educational, social and later-life contexts due to a lack of support from society predominantly. This is why it is imperative to challenge neuronormativity in schools, as it creates harmful biases against neurodivergent children, which may negatively impact the notion of inclusion. This may result in neurodivergent children facing increased rates of discrimination, exclusion and bullying in school.

The inclusion and acceptance of neurodiverse children in your school creates a place of unique strengths and perspectives that contribute towards diverse problem-solving, creativity and forms of innovation. Without neurodiversity, we would miss out on opportunities for the contributions of these children. Schools should endeavour to appreciate and recognise the full range of neurological differences present in society. Through the promotion of neurodiversity, we create an inclusive school environment for neurodivergent children to flourish.

REFLECTION 5.1

Reflect on your own teaching styles and pedagogy.

Can you think of some ways in which you may have inadvertently promoted neuronormativity?

How might you revise some pedagogy and teaching habits to be more inclusive and challenge ableism?

SEPARATION OF SEN AND DISABILITY

The SEN *Code of Practice* (DfE and DoH, 2015) defines a child as having special educational needs due to a learning difficulty or disability if they have significantly greater difficulty in learning than the majority of their peers or have a disability that hinders them from making use of facilities provided in mainstream schools. In addition, SEN children may also have a disability under the Equality Act (2010).

Contrary to common belief, SEN and disabilities hold differing definitions. SEN in school refers to whether a child has special educational needs, or if they have a learning difficulty/disability which requires a special provision to make education more accessible.

5 Challenging ableism and neuronormativity

Examples of some of the most common SEN are:

- emotional and behavioural difficulties;

- autism and Asperger syndrome;

- attention deficit (hyperactivity) disorder (ADD/ADHD);

- specific learning difficulties;

- obsessive compulsive disorder (OCD);

- communication difficulties;

- medical needs such as epilepsy and cerebral palsy;

- mobility difficulties.

Disability, however, can be referred to as a physical or mental impairment, as examined in Chapter 4. But not all disabled children require special educational support. It is a common misconception that SEN and disability are one entity, but this is not always the case. Children with SEN can have a disability and vice versa, but they may not. Furthermore, while SEN and disability are not synonymous, they are very often a joint combination of issues – for example, a child who is wheelchair bound may develop a mental health issue due to dealing with their physical difficulties.

It is widely understood that children with SEN and/or disabilities may have increased difficulties when learning. Therefore, the SEN *Code of Practice* (DfE and DoH, 2015) defines these learning needs through four broad areas of need:

- communication and interaction;

- cognition and learning;

- social, emotional and mental health difficulties;

- sensory and/or physical needs.

SEN IN SCHOOLS

There are various degrees of support available in schools for children with SEN. These come in the form of school-implemented SEN plans and EHCPs, which may be carried out by assessment through your local authority. You will experience working with both types of support throughout your teaching career.

SEN PLANS

SEN support plans are created and maintained by the school and SENCO, outlining the additional support the child is to receive while in school. This may include a special learning programme, extra help from a teaching assistant (TA), observation during break times, extra encouragement in their learning, etc. The child's school is responsible for maintaining and adjusting a SEN plan throughout the year, ensuring it is kept accurate for the child's needs. Across all primary schools in England, there are 14.1 per cent of pupils receiving an SEN support plan. The current most common type of need among these children are speech, language and communication needs (gov.uk, 2024).

EDUCATIONAL HEALTH CARE PLANS

Education health care plans (EHCPs) are available for children who require more support than is available through SEN support within the school. An EHCP identifies educational, health and social needs, while setting out additional support to help meet the needs of these children. It follows a statutory assessment process involving external support agencies such as local authority-based education support, educational psychologists and behaviour management consultants, etc., further identifying long-term outcomes. According to recent figures (gov.uk, 2024), 3 per cent of primary children have an EHCP, which is an increase from the previous year, with children on the autistic spectrum making up a third of the children in receipt of an EHCP. Overall, there were an additional 18,900 pupils with plans in 2023.

IDENTIFIED CONDITIONS LEADING TO SEN SUPPORT

There are a multitude of conditions which may result in a child requiring SEN support while attending school. These are listed and discussed in Table 5.1, with the total number of children recorded as receiving support, both EHCP and SEN support plans in school (gov.uk, 2024).

Table 5.1 Total number of children receiving support, both EHCP and SEN support plans in school (gov.uk, 2024)

Condition	SEN support	EHCP
Autistic spectrum disorder	104,395	132,249
Hearing impairment	17,156	6,320
Moderate learning difficulty	179,156	33,954
Multisensory impairment	3,312	1,261
Other difficulty/disability	42,153	8,734
Physical disability	21,872	14,568

(Continued)

5 Challenging ableism and neuronormativity

Table 5.1 (Continued)

Condition	SEN support	EHCP
Profound and multiple learning difficulty	780	10,014
No assessment of type of need	53,641	–
Severe learning difficulty	2,193	31,787
Social, emotional and mental health	254,202	62,125
Specific learning difficulty	158,974	17,361
Speech, language and communications need	291,742	78,199
Visual impairment	9,766	3,835
Total	1,139,746	400,413

CASE STUDY 5.1

Challenging the impact of ableism and neuronormativity in the classroom

David, the head teacher of a primary school located in Merseyside in the North West of England, recognises inclusion as an important aspect of educational systems around the world. He places a high priority on ensuring children with SEN have access to mainstream education. He is aware of the stereotypes and misconceptions which can misinform assumptions that students with disabilities or neurodiverse conditions are less capable. Often use of derogatory language or negative attitudes towards students with disabilities or neurodiverse conditions can create a language environment fuelled with negativity. He knows that, if left unchecked, these systemic barriers silently facilitated by notions of ableism and neuronormativity can lead to lack of accommodations, rigid teaching methods and inflexible policies that do not consider diverse learning needs over time. The impact on students can not only be limited academic achievement, but also poor mental health and problems with social integration in the long run.

His senior leadership team and teaching staff believe that the right for children with SEN to receive education in mainstream schools alongside their peers is important, and vital with regard to the right to have equal opportunities to participate. This is why David promotes a learner-centred teaching approach, meaning the children's needs are at the forefront of the school. Throughout his years as head teacher, David has found that children with SEN attending his primary school have tended to perform as well or to a higher academic level when compared to children with SEN attending a local specialised school in the area.

David and his senior team believe that this success is down to their school's ethos of treating everyone equally. This implies both socially and academically. Children of all abilities are held to the same standards and expectations. He states that his teaching staff hold very high expectations of all children, and they foster an increased focus on academic achievement in their school. David asked his staff to discuss their thoughts on their academic success with SEN children in mainstream schooling during a staff meeting. Many staff referred to the supportive classroom climate, expectations of child performance and the cognitive and/or the social-emotional dimensions that the teachers foster in the classroom. The cognitive dimension includes guiding the children's learning, assessing progress and providing adequate support. The socio-emotional dimension is in reference to teachers being supportive and positive, fostering a strong relationship between teacher and child. David concluded the staff meeting by recognising and praising the work and support of all his staff.

During the staff meeting, some staff raised concerns of anxiety over their knowledge to fully support all children with SEN in their classroom. David took this on board and planned consecutive workshops of appropriate SEN-focused CPD sessions for all the staff. These focused on strategies to help develop SEN children's academic and social skills in a supportive and learner-centred manner. David was recommended the Whole School SEND website (www.wholeschoolsend.org.uk/) by the head teacher from the local special school as a useful resource to help provide his staff with additional support to develop their SEN understanding.

Staff were asked to take the information on board and implement some of the suggested strategies during class for the next few weeks of the half-term. Teachers implemented some of the following strategies in their classrooms.

- Tailoring the teaching methods to meet the needs of the children by differentiating teaching. This ensured that all children could fully access the curriculum being taught.

- Empowering children by asking the child how best the teacher could help them. Teachers understood that getting suggestions from the learner is good practice in teaching children to advocate for their needs.

- Developing discussions with the parents or caregiver. Making use of the people close to the child helped develop their understanding of SEN pupils' needs as a whole. Teachers also understood that there might be more additional needs prevalent at home that they may not be aware of in school.

- Incorporated feedback mechanisms in their teaching. Asking the children or parents to provide feedback on the support being implemented was a good starter for reflection and development in their own SEN knowledge and strategy toolkit.

- Teachers explored the SEN systems already in place in the school; they challenged anything they felt should be developed and stated why. They realised that this might be a hiccup in the system which could be smoothed further.

Another staff meeting was arranged to discuss the strategies and consequences of implementation to help deepen the class teachers' knowledge and support of SEN children. This feedback was further collected on a staff Padlet for future reference and implementation in the classroom. David viewed this as an appropriate resource for teachers to use and add to when needed.

> ┌─ **REFLECTION 5.2** ─────────────────────────────
> │
> │ Think about the strategies listed above.
> │
> │ How could you use these strategies to develop your understanding of challenging ableism
> │ and neuronormativity in your school?
> └──

RESPONSIBILITY FOR SEN CHILDREN

Teachers are an influential figure in a SEN child's education and social life; they provide a safe space for these children to develop in a range of areas. However, many mainstream teachers often feel ill prepared to accommodate and teach SEN children and this can be attributed as one of the key reasons for the underachievement of SEN children in mainstream schools. It is evident that the education system cannot be better than the quality of teachers operating in it, including the quality of SEN-related content knowledge. This is not a new issue as it has been evident for quite some time, yet real change has only been recently brought about through the SEN and Alternative Provision Green Paper published in 2022. The number of SEN children in the education system in 2024 is 18.4 per cent (gov. uk, 2024) so it is clear that all teachers will teach children with SEN throughout their career. Therefore, all teachers should be equipped with a basic understanding of SEN which allows them to identify and deal with challenges productively in their classroom.

A survey of teachers conducted by Hartley and the National Association for Special Educational Needs (2010) found 73 per cent of respondents stated that they found it difficult to recruit specialist SEN staff. On average, the survey exposed that per school only 52 per cent of teachers had a qualification in SEN, with only 30 per cent holding a relevant qualification regarding the particular needs of the children they were teaching. Additionally, only 34 per cent of teaching support staff had any qualification in SEN. These percentages have only increased over time. In the Pearson *School Report* (2024), 61 per cent of respondents stated the prevalence of SEN is of increasing concern as there is a lack of specialist provision and outreach expertise, leaving many children without sufficient support to thrive. This report indicated that SEN was the top barrier for pupil learning in primary school, with 83 per cent of respondents agreeing.

Currently, the issues these findings highlight are being addressed through the creation of a *golden thread* through ITT, through to early career support and onto school leadership. The overall aim of this golden thread is to support teachers with high-quality training and development and improve outcomes for all children, including those with SEND, in special and mainstream schools. The impact of this policy is yet to be seen as it is too early to measure. In addition to the above, schools can focus on providing targeted CPD for in-service teachers to progress their skills from time to time during their careers.

Teachers should be encouraged to identify gaps in their skills and knowledge that are not sufficient to provide for SEN children and they should discuss further steps with their school SENCO. Often professionally qualified SENCOs hold specialised knowledge on SEN along with considerable practical experience and are able to direct class teachers in the right direction.

The *Code of Practice* (DfE and DoH, 2015) says that every teacher is a teacher of SEN. It says that 'Class and subject teachers, supported by the senior leadership team, should make regular assessments of progress for all pupils' (p. 95). Where concerns are identified, teachers should work with the SENCO to assess whether the child has SEN. Teachers should set clear progress targets for all pupils with SEN that focus on their potential to achieve at or above expectation.

Although teachers are a key part of the support for their pupils, there are many other bodies responsible for a SEN child's development. These include parents, carers, the school SENCO, local authorities, the NHS and, finally, the DfE. There is a range of contributing institutions responsible for the child's achievement and development while they are attending school.

WHAT DO THE POLICIES SAY?

The *Special Educational Needs and Disability Code of Practice: 0 to 25 Years* (DfE and DoH, 2015) is a statutory guidance document which aims to support those working with SEN children. Although dated, this document is the forefront of information regarding the duties, policies and procedures which relate to Part 3 of the Children and Families Act (2014). Local authorities, schools and the NHS must regard this guidance and it should be evident in your school.

Since the previous SEN *Code of Practice*, there have been multiple changes which will be explored here. The 2015 edition covers an age range of 0–25 years, and includes further guidance on disabled children alongside those with SEN. The new statutory policy indicates more guidance to be given for education and training services to help educational professionals identify and support children with SEN. According to the 2015 guidance, teachers should have an increased focus on support which enables children with SEN to succeed.

There are three principles that underpin the SEN *Code of Practice* (DfE and DoH, 2015), as outlined in the Children and Families Act. These are:

1. having a regard for the views and feelings of the child and their parents;

2. making the child a priority while ensuring they participate in all decisions fully;

3. providing the correct support in order for the facilitation of development.

These principles have been designed to promote: child participation; early identification; more choice and control for the child; collaboration between services providing support; ensuring accurate provision is in place; inclusive education and practice for SEN children; and to prepare the child for adulthood – for example, independent living or future employment prospects. Appropriate implementation of these principles should result in reduction of the negative impact notions linked with ableism and neuronormativity can have on the educational attainment of SEN children.

Many SEN children feel misunderstood due to ableism and may believe that people do not value them. Including their thoughts and opinions is vital in ensuring they feel heard and appreciated. One of the many benefits of including the child and parents in decision-making is the increased fit of the needs and services provided. In turn, this should lead to higher rates of satisfaction and reduced costs as the long-term benefits emerge over time. It should be noted that effective participation happens when it is valued, planned and resourced correctly. It should be evident in all stages of the planning and monitoring of support systems put in place for the child in your school. Each member of the family, including the child, should be aware of their role in the scenario and how best to provide for the child. Implementing effective participation will result in strong feedback systems which will ensure that the child and family understand and agree with the support being provided.

Regardless of the policies put in place to ensure there is appropriate support for children with SEN, many parents and children feel frustrated by the system and feel as though they constantly battle to access support. The SEN and Alternative Provision Green Paper (2022) set out proposals to deliver change for a more inclusive system after deep-diving into the issues present in the old SEN system. With another plan published in 2023, the system has been further challenged to improve. The foundation of a new SEN and Alternative Provision system will increase clarity and improve mainstream provision, giving more children the support they need in their local setting. Additionally, it will reduce the need to access additional support through EHCPs. The new system will be built upon national standards, which are set to be published by the end of 2025, with an increased budget to fund new places in specialist schools and existing provision for children. The hope is that this new system will bring about a more positive experience for children with SEN and their families, while creating a more inclusive society that celebrates and provides opportunities for every child to succeed.

ROLE OF INCLUSIVE EDUCATIONAL PRACTICES IN CHALLENGING ABLEISM AND NEURONORMATIVITY

Inclusion in education is a basic human right and is the foundation of the development of a more just and equal society. Inclusion in education refers to all children learning in an environment that respects children regardless of gender, race, ethnicity, ability or disability

(UNESCO, 2009). An inclusive education works to identify all the barriers facing children in education, endeavouring to remove them to ensure the entire curriculum is covered in depth for all children. It focuses on including all children to access equal opportunities of education and learning.

Just as each child's needs are different, the impact of their SEN on learning can vary. Children may experience both academic and social barriers due to their SEN, meaning they are unable to reach their full potential while in school. Without the correct support being implemented, those barriers could cause an increase in disengagement, frustration and challenging behaviours within school. These behaviours may include:

- withdrawn behaviours such as anxiety, school phobia and social isolation;

- disruptive behaviours such as shouting out, angry outbursts, screaming and refusing to follow the class instructions from the teacher;

- violent or unsafe behaviours such as physically harming themselves or others, running away or damaging school or individual property.

By effectively supporting SEN in the classroom through tailoring your learning environment and pedagogy to become more inclusive, you can ensure that these barriers to learning are reduced. Remember, a child's area of need may evolve during their journey through your school; some children may have fluctuating needs. For example, an intervention to reduce social anxiety could lead to these issues being addressed, bringing the skills back in line with their age expectancy.

For your school to fully embrace an inclusive education, teachers can make adaptations to physical spaces in school to ensure all children are able to access all resources, as well as the daily school routines such as teaching pedagogy and classroom rules. For example, some children with severe SEN may require a reduced or adapted timetable, with different start and finish times compared to their peers. Other children may need specialist equipment such as communication devices to communicate their learning or dialogue with teachers and peers. Others may require the use of sensory rooms or quiet spaces to help regulate their emotions when feeling overwhelmed or stressed. It is possible that your school may feel it necessary to hire additional staff to provide further support for children with SEN.

When education is truly inclusive, it can have consequential benefits for all children, not just those who have SEN. Studies have found that an inclusive education has been recognised in promoting friendships, improving communication skills, encouraging the development of social skills with everyone. Often children with SEN report having fewer friends than their peers and are observed to have fewer opportunities for interaction with children of a similar age (Koster et al., 2010). Children with SEN are twice as likely to be consistently absent from school, and they are eight times as likely to be excluded from school. Inclusive education schools have higher levels of skills and achievement in children with additional needs, but there is also evidence suggesting that inclusive education schools have fewer absences or referrals due to inappropriate behaviour.

REFLECTION 5.3

Think about the inclusion strategies your school is currently using.

Do you feel they represent all children, including the inclusion of children with SEN?

Does your school have positive outcomes for all children due to the inclusion strategies - for example, the promotion of friendships between neurotypical and neurodiverse children?

ISSUES ARISING FROM INCLUSION AND 'LABELLING'

Identifying a child's special education needs provides an opportunity for schools to further support them in their learning; however, some parents may have concerns regarding the possible consequences of labelling their child as SEN. A SEN label may lead to stigma. Stigma is a negative attitude towards a person, which may eventually develop into discrimination and exclusion in school. In a less educated society, when people hear the words 'special educational needs', they tend to think of children with severe physical and mental needs, rather than a child whose needs are less severe. In this context, the word 'special' implies that these children are different and therefore lesser than their peers. This mindset leads to discrimination and a lack of access to peers, peer events and education for both the children and their families, with an overall decline in the child's mental health and self-esteem.

Parents are aware that a child with SEN may additionally be labelled as slow or incapable, regardless of whether they learn at the same pace as their peers, or even excel in some areas of the curriculum. For example, a child might have a speech delay that means it takes longer for them to speak up during class, with many peers viewing this child as slow academically, even if this view is inaccurate. A child with Down syndrome may be viewed as having delayed mental and physical development which may negatively inform their peers of the child's ability. However, this is not accurate as a child with Down syndrome might be academically brighter than average. It is important to remember that a person's ability or inability is not defined by their diagnosis.

INCLUSIVE STRATEGIES TO SUPPORT CHILDREN WITH SEN

Every school is required to have systems in place to identify children who need additional support, through assessment, monitoring and securing appropriate support. Under the *Code of Practice* (DfE and DoH, 2015), schools must:

- make sure children with SEN receive the support they need; schools should be doing everything they can to meet children's SEN requirements;

- have a designated teacher who is responsible for coordinating SEN provision (the SENCO);

- keep parents informed when making special educational provisions for children;

- create and prepare SEN support plans as outlined previously in the chapter.

Throughout any decisions regarding support for children with SEN, schools must keep parents involved during the process. Schools receive additional funding to help provide support for SEN children, known as a delegated budget. Each child with SEN is entitled to receive up to £6,000 per annum (at the time of writing).

There is an abundance of resources available online with suggestions of inclusive strategies to help support children with SEN in your classroom. Below are some ideas and teaching strategies that you can easily integrate into your classroom to support children with SEN, regardless of cost or staff shortages which are facing the education system today. Some useful resources have been included in the Further reading section at the end of the chapter.

CREATE A POSITIVE AND SUPPORTIVE LEARNING ENVIRONMENT

Careful consideration of how your classroom is organised can significantly support learners with SEN in the classroom and remove potential barriers to learning. This might include limiting classroom displays which will decrease sensory overloads, avoiding black on white presentations and varying the background colour when using PowerPoint or slides. It is important to teach children about well-being and mental health. It may be beneficial to introduce a class feelings board – for example, *zones of regulation* – as part of the daily class routine. Providing a visual aid such as timetables makes it more accessible for SEN children. It might be useful to make an independent workstation available to children to use when necessary; having a quiet space may be beneficial for some learners.

UNDERSTAND PUPILS AND THEIR NEEDS

When you feel overwhelmed, make sure to ask for advice from colleagues or your school SENCO. The SENCO has access to information for each child and will be able to provide appropriate suggestions depending on the individual child's needs. Ensure you are in communication with SEN children's parents; if needs be, a home–school contact book is a good alternative if time for conversations is limited. Different children have different needs when learning, so it is important to have the correct classroom equipment to accommodate this. Your SENCO will be able to advise you on what additional equipment is necessary, but some examples include:

- writing slopes

- specialised pencil grips

- ear defenders

- wobble cushions

- task management board

- fidget toys.

CONTINUALLY EVALUATE YOUR TEACHING

While teaching, remain open-minded to the possibility of changing pedagogy style to suit the children's learning needs. Make use of available CPD opportunities to enhance your knowledge of support for children with SEN. Always remember, what works for one child during a lesson may not work for the next – be prepared to change! If you feel you need additional support with SEN children in your class, make use of available time for discussions with your school SENCO and senior leadership team. There are structures and people in place in school who are available to provide additional support and knowledge to help you; do make use of them. Adjusting your teaching style does not mean you are an ineffective teacher; it is a normal adapting process to best suit the needs of the learners in your classroom.

ENSURE THAT ALL CHILDREN HAVE ACCESS TO HIGH-QUALITY TEACHING

It is common practice to use differentiated tasks for children with varied abilities; this allows children of a lower ability to progress their learning at their rate. It may be beneficial to implement the use of *talk partners*; this provides SEN children opportunities to engage and interact with peers, allowing them to practise their answers with peer support. Here are some key features to ensure that SEN children can access high-quality teaching:

1. keep instructions clear and concise;

2. deliver instructions facing the children;

3. do not issue multiple instructions at once;

4. give children an opportunity to repeat instructions back to you;

5. accompany verbal instructions with visual aids (symbols, images, or even Makaton signs);

6. when appropriate, an adult can reword or rephrase instructions for certain children;

7. make sure to verbalise your thought process when modelling activities and include help strategies;

8. avoid idiomatic language as some children may take it literally.

USE CAREFULLY SELECTED SMALL-GROUP AND ONE-TO-ONE INTERVENTIONS

You will most likely have children in your class who require access to intervention to help fulfil their full potential, in addition to the high-quality whole-class teaching that you are providing. Your SENCO will be able to advise you on which interventions would best meet the needs of each child, as well as advising on who is best to complete the intervention. Interventions should be completed during an agreed time slot, accompanied by goals to be completed, and regularly evaluated. All learners have a statutory right to a broad and balanced curriculum, so care must be taken to ensure that children with SEN are not consistently removed from lessons for interventions. For example, always completing interventions during assembly time would deny the child inclusion in a valuable and memorable part of school life.

WORK EFFECTIVELY WITH TEACHING ASSISTANTS

Teaching assistants (TAs) are an essential part of supporting children with SEN while learning, alongside teachers. Many TAs can provide additional support in the classroom such as delivering interventions or providing small-group work when completing tasks. You should involve your TA, if you have one, in the planning and evaluation process of SEN children and they should be provided with time, training and the resources necessary to prepare for their role during lesson times. Previously, there have been tendencies to place a TA directly one-to-one with a SEN child, but this does not foster independence or promote inclusion in your classroom. Instead, teachers and TA should endeavour to work as a team to provide high-quality, targeted support.

TEACHING ABOUT SEN

Ensuring that you as a teacher are challenging the notions of ableism and neuronormativity, as well as supporting children with SEN in your classroom, is an important factor in your class understanding the challenges facing some of their peers. It is equally important to teach them about ableism and neuronormativity so they can understand that not everyone is the same, and not everyone has the same needs. For example, when delivering the main teaching input, you may provide fidget toys to children who require them, such as children with autism, to help maintain their concentration. Some children may question your choice and lack the understanding that their peer is not being given a toy to play with, but a tool to help them concentrate and learn. Children may not understand your choices for additional support, if it is not explained and given context in their terms. A great way to discuss SEN with children is by discussing the impact some children face if they have SEN. It is important to address your class's questions because at some point they will come across a person or peer with SEN; how you respond is likely to affect the way these children view SEN. It is the perfect opportunity for you to foster an attitude of inclusion and acceptance in your classroom. You may also want to encourage SEN children in your class to take part in these important discussions, providing a unique opinion on their experience. We have bullet pointed some starting points for you to use below:

- address their curiosity, but be factual;

- be sensitive when discussing the topic of SEN. Some children in your class may have family members with SEN, even if there are no SEN children in your class;

- no two people are the same; some people have differences which appear to be more noticeable;

- SEN is a characteristic of a person. They will have similar qualities to other children such as likes and dislikes, strengths and challenges; emphasise the similarities between them;

- children with SEN are like all children – they want to make friends, be included and respected;

- children can be born with SEN, or others may develop SEN after an accident or illness;

- children with SEN can still do the same things that all children want to do, it just might take them slightly longer. Sometimes a child with SEN may need some extra help from an adult or equipment to help them.

REFLECTION 5.4

Think about the inclusion strategies discussed above.

How do you think your school could implement these strategies to support children with SEN in your classroom?

As a school, how well do you do at supporting all children with SEN, including children with more complex needs?

CONCLUSION

This chapter has given you an insight into the world built in favour of ableism and neuronormativity. Your role as an inclusive teacher is to challenge these notions and advocate for a more inclusive and accepting society. The first steps towards this are in your classroom. Teaching and normalising neurodiversity in your classroom with children of a range of abilities will change their preconceived perspective into a more understanding and accepting tone. Children should be taught that children with SEN are human, but with different characteristics. We have provided you with a bank of strategies that you may wish to implement in your classroom to help support learners with SEN, making your classroom a supportive and welcoming environment for these children. As teachers, it is vital for us to provide for all children, even if it means asking for extra help from support staff or your school SENCO. It may take more time to prepare for lessons to ensure all children are provided for, but in doing so we will create a positive environment in which all children can flourish both socially and academically.

CHAPTER SUMMARY

Considering what we have explored, within this chapter we have covered:

- how SEN and disability are not synonymous and explored their differences;
- key policy developments relating to the current context of SEN in schools;
- the role of inclusive educational practices in challenging ableism and neuronormativity;
- policies that have influenced SEN practice, alongside possible dilemmas surrounding labelling children as SEN;
- discussed some best practice initiatives to support children with SEN.

FURTHER READING AND RESOURCES

6 Teaching Strategies for SEN Pupils

www.janets.org.uk/teaching-strategies-for-SEN-pupils/

This website highlights six strategies which you can easily implement in your classroom to help SEN children receive a regular mainstream education in an adapted classroom setting. It provides detailed descriptions of each strategy, which have been widely recognised and used across the UK.

Supporting Children with Special Education Needs and Disabilities Podcast

High Speed Training

https://open.spotify.com/episode/1IxTtS55rYxLrSHOJ3SQDa

This podcast follows the notion that there is no 'one size fits all' approach to supporting children with SEN. It discusses strategies such as implementing a positive and inclusive learning environment, good general practice, high-quality teaching; many more areas are addressed throughout the podcast.

5 Challenging ableism and neuronormativity

Don't Call Me Special by Pat Thomas

This children's book is about children who have different disabilities which range from physical disabilities to learning disabilities. It shows how these children cope with it daily while participating in normal sports and classroom activities. The book answers many questions and possible concerns children may have about others with disabilities or SEN. It teaches children the correct way to interact with their friends who may be different from them.

A Practical Guide to Special Educational Needs in Inclusive Primary Classrooms by Richard Rose and Marie Howley

This book is written for teachers; it is a practical and accessible introduction to working with children of a range of abilities in an inclusive primary classroom. It is informed by research regarding SEN children and provides examples and advice on how to meet the challenges of developing effective teaching and learning in inclusive settings.

My Brain is Magic: A Sensory-Seeking Celebration by Prasha Sooful

This children's book shines a light on neurodiversity and the sensory process in a full and accessible way for all children to enjoy.

We Move Together by Kelly Fritsch and Anne McGuire

This children's book is a bold yet colourful exploration of all the ways people navigate through life, and a celebration of the relationships fostered along the way. It follows a mixed-ability group of children as they creatively negotiate everyday barriers and find joy through a disability culture and community.

6
COMMUNAL IDENTITY
AMY BOYD

> **THIS CHAPTER**
>
> The chapter will provide opportunities for readers to reflect upon:
>
> - why communal identity is important in schools
> - whole-school events which could be used to establish a positive communal identity
> - opportunities in different subject areas which can be used to develop children's connection with *people* and *place.*

DEFINITIONS

To begin this chapter, it is important to determine some of the key definitions that are used throughout.

- *Communal identity*: this can be identified through the observation of a group's communal activities, rituals, rites and holiday celebrations. It is a collective identity that indicates the particularity and distinguishing features of the community.

- *Social identity*: this can be defined as an individual's knowledge of belonging to certain social groups, alongside emotional and valuational significance of this membership. It is the part of the self-concept that derives from group membership.

- *In-groups*: these can be defined as groups of people or things that are united by a common trait. They are social groups to which an individual psychologically identifies as being a member.

- *Out-groups*: these are social groups that an individual does not identify with. The individual does not feel united by a common trait.

- *Cultural engagement*: this is the notion of all children feeling welcomed and accepted. It may include the school's engagement and appreciation towards the different cultures present in the school community.

6 Communal identity

INTRODUCTION

Communal identity is the lens through which members of groups and societies view themselves and others. Before attending school, children are exposed to and participate in a range of communities outside their families such as neighbourhoods, religious organisations, day-care or playschools. Children will have acquired a sense of communal identity separately from the school environment. It is important to acknowledge these through supportive pedagogies; communal identity can be affected both positively and negatively in the classroom, based on stereotypes, associations and memories.

Individuals will construct their identities depending on others – more understandably, their perception of the *other*. This reiterates the thought that identity can be assumed as the sense of self in relation to other individuals. Moreover, schools should express that identity may further focus on the differences between individuals. All of this contributes towards a school's ethos regarding cultural engagement. Cultural engagement is often defined as students of all cultures feeling accepted and welcomed in the learning environment. It can also include the institution's engagement with different cultures both within the staff–student body and in the local or global community. Hess et al. state that cultural engagement occurs when there are reciprocal relations between faculty members, community partners and students (Hess et al., 2007).

This chapter will explore the formation of communal identity, including the intergroup comparison of in-group and out-groups when applied to the school environment. We will discuss what is meant by the term 'school communal identity' and cultural engagement, before, finally, exploring how to promote a sense of belonging and identity through subject inclusion of the curriculum and cultural engagement strategies which can be implemented in your school.

FORMATION OF COMMUNAL IDENTITY

Identity is a multilayered and contextual aspect, constituted of cultural, social and personal elements. Identity development is therefore a consequence of social communities. Communities are centred on a common interest, with a shared purpose that unites members to collectively pursue an unachievable aim as individual members. Remember, sometimes our identity is subconscious, meaning that we might not realise we identify as or with something until we are forced to acknowledge it!

A school is a cultural institution where the policies, curriculum, pedagogical practices, values, forms of communication with parents and local communities are framed by social practices (Hjörne et al., 2012). Therefore, a school can be viewed as a community in itself, with shared practices contributing to the development of the school's context. The school communal identity may mean different things as a teacher or learner, due to the different

84

responsibilities both entail. As a teacher, your communal identity may closely align with other teachers, fostering the feeling of respect and responsibility, yet care for the children. A child's communal identity as a learner may focus on their experiences during school lessons and time with peers. Outside school, children are exposed to various social identities which become intertwined with identity formation. Children may develop different competencies, skills and further knowledge that inform their personal identity. Within schools, individual children's independent experience may or may not be acknowledged; either in the form of value and appreciation or kept as a private matter. This provides an opportunity for classrooms to display these individualised assets.

Communal identity contributes towards the formation of personal identity. This in turn forms a social identity which leads to a development in social categorisation. This social categorisation is defined through distinct social groups, known as *in-groups* and *out-groups*, creating an intergroup comparison based on identity. As a consequence, individuals may feel satisfied or dissatisfied with their intergroup comparison basis. This theory is known as Tajfel's theory of social identity (1979). Although dated, it is still applicable to modern-day identity formation.

REFLECTION 6.1

Reflect upon your identity as a teacher in school and how it may contribute towards your sense of communal identity.

IN-GROUP AND OUT-GROUP SEPARATION

Social identity theory asserts that an individual's sense of self is determined by the groups which they belong to, rather than by their individuality. The sense of self is underpinned through an internal sense of social identity, causing behaviours which are typical of group traits. These characteristics are a consequence of individuals maintaining a positive view through differentiating in-groups from out-groups. This view of groups creates an environment where individuals think in terms of 'we' and 'us' rather than 'I'. Groups wish to view 'us' as different or better than 'them' in order to feel accomplished in who they, as a group, are (Bizumic et al., 2017). Achieving this accomplished feeling is not always manageable for members of low-status groups (such as those deemed as 'unpopular'), reaffirming their sense of inferior status.

Social identity theory is based on group association to help form our conception of self-identity, which helps produce our sense of association with groups. Social identity can foster feelings of belonging, purpose, self-worth and identity. Research indicates that feelings of discrimination may be formed through a sense of favouritism towards personal groups rather than the view of negative feelings towards other groups. This notion is known as intergroup bias; it can be broken down to in-group favouritism and out-group discrimination. An in-group is a group which an individual belongs to, compared to an out-group, meaning the individual does not belong. The theory asserts that people have natural tendencies to perceive their in-group in a more positive light compared to being either neutral or negative towards out-groups, increasing their sense of identity. It is important to acknowledge that in-groups and out-groups are fluid concepts, meaning that a person's group and identity may evolve and change based on context, environment and over time. A person may also belong to multiple in-groups across different facets of their identity. Examples of these are listed in Table 6.1.

Table 6.1   Facets of identity

Facets of identity	In-group examples	Out-group examples
Ethnicity and race	Someone of an Asian ethnicity may identify with other Asian people	The same individual may view white, black or native American people as an out-group
Religion	Muslims may identify with other Muslims	A Muslim may perceive Christians, Hindus or Buddhists as out-groups
Nationality	An American might feel a close association with other Americans	To an American, individuals from Canada, Mexico and Brazil might be viewed as out-groups
Profession	Teachers may feel linked to other teachers	Different professions such as lawyers, doctors or bricklayers may be seen as out-groups
Gender and sexual orientation	Individuals who identify as LGBTQ+ might feel a sense of community with others who identify the same	Individuals who identify as heterosexual might be viewed as out-groups to those individuals

COMMUNAL SCHOOL IDENTITY

School identities, from a socio-cultural theory perspective, are not primarily formed as a result of innate traits of family, culture and outside-school practices; rather an influential factor is the school's discourse of practices and leadership hierarchy. A child's physical presentations – for example, their school uniform – often contribute to their school identities, with an individual's race and ethnicity becoming more apparent as they become older. Classrooms provide a stimulating, yet interactive environment for individuals to develop their identities, through forms of display and participation. These forms may also contribute to a communal identity, as explored further in this chapter, indicating that identity is not developed in present time but through past experiences, within the frame of language. It is important to acknowledge that western countries' teaching and learning is dissimilar to other cultures. A contemporary materialistic definition of school identity focuses on the correlation between physical presentation and movement with clothing, racial characteristics, classrooms, curriculum guides, resources. Resources in schools may be limited due to funding; however, a simple instance of using scissors in the classroom may lead to someone's identity feeling undervalued. For example, if right-handed scissors are the only scissors available in a classroom it can make left-handed pupils feel incompetent. Materials and resources in classrooms matter; teachers should try to provide, where possible, the resources needed for children to succeed with limited challenges. All these factors contribute towards a child's school identity and therefore the school's communal identity.

REFLECTION 6.2

Do you feel your school adequately prepares children's identities to be valued, leading to an increased sense of communal identity in school?

If not, how do you think they could be better prepared? Think about clothing alternatives, resources and classroom materials.

It is widely recognised that schools portray unique 'personalities', meaning a set of shared normalities, values and beliefs which define the school's ethos. This may be more commonly referred to as the school *climate*, a term used to describe features within the school environment (Thapa et al., 2013). This construct is multidimensional, measured through staff support for the school's objectives, fairness and consistency when implementing the school rules, academic priorities and respectful relationships between staff children, parents and the local community. School community and feelings of connectedness have been defined as the belief that both pupils and adults in school care about each other and the learning taking place in school.

The sense of belonging a child feels at school can be assessed in terms of whether they feel happy, safe, fairly treated and valued. The sense of belonging is pivotal to a child's success at school, all these aspects relate to a sense of care and respect towards learning. It is necessary to understand the school's norms, values and beliefs and instil them into your classroom climate to ensure all children feel like they belong and are appreciated.

CULTURAL ENGAGEMENT

Cultural engagement allows schools to provide enrichment for children to partake in cultural activities, adding beneficial well-being time. It enlists a sense of tolerance and pride for those in the school community who are different from oneself, promoting a sense of welcome and belongingness. The development of cultural engagement enhances the feeling of a communal identity within the school.

Cultural engagement plays a vital role in the development of an effective school. It promotes a feeling of inclusivity, which in turn brings about feelings of happiness, safety, sense of

6 Communal identity

community and, lastly but most importantly, it has positive impacts on children's learning both in the classroom and socially. It is crucial in creating a welcoming atmosphere for refugee and immigrant children, along with children from more diverse cultural backgrounds. The spotlight below outlines the necessity of cultural engagement in schools ...

CASE STUDY 6.1

Inclusion and belonging in London schools

In 2023, the University of Bath alongside London's Violence Reduction Unit, conducted a study based on inclusion and belonging in London schools. Findings from this research highlight the fundamental importance of a secure sense of belonging and safety to children's inclusion in education. Students identified respect, fairness and being listened to as vital features of the caring, nurturing relationships needed to feel included in school. This study found that 66 per cent of primary-aged children felt a sense of belonging in school. Notably one child stated that their school has a range of pupils from various backgrounds and countries, and that teachers endeavour to discuss these contexts (Brown et al., 2024). One of the main barriers to belonging was identified as schools not recognising children's identities; 36 per cent of primary-aged pupils stated that being incapable of being themselves in school was the top factor. Many children connected this feeling with the school's lack of understanding of different types of people.

The research conducted above stated that a lack of value in children's identities creates an environment which may have lasting impacts for marginalised children. However, it is important to remember that research also suggests lacking a sense of belonging in education settings does not have to be continual throughout a child's whole school career (Sanders and Munford, 2016). Schools have the potential to be game changers in the lives of vulnerable children particularly. Suggested recommendations were to recognise the value of developing and acknowledging equity and diversity in the school population. Teachers should also recognise and focus attention upon the ways that students' lives outside school influence their behaviours at school. Such caring relationships do not reduce the sense of being different, but they certainly reduce the power the sense of difference has to undermine the construction of a positive sense of identity in school. This incorporates synthesising school policies with the insurance that all children feel welcomed and valued, while considering the needs of different cultures and faiths. Implementing such inclusive strategies involves providing opportunities to explore and add value to our differences, encouraging children to challenge the stereotypes which lead to racism and discrimination.

A connected community between children, teachers, leaders and the wider school will promote a positive environment of belonging and purpose. Examples of this cultural enrichment include hosting external events for the local community to celebrate the different world cultures and festivals, or embedding cultural enrichment in the curriculum taught in schools; suggested examples are discussed in the next section.

SUBJECT INCLUSION

Teaching cultural elements, such as texts, music, films, artefacts and similar sculptures, should be an educational aim of primary schools (Hjörne et al., 2012) as cultural elements are fundamental. Cultural elements are a source of knowledge which may foster a form of social cohesion between individuals and are expected to contribute to both children's intellectual and emotional development. It remains comprehensible that in school taught curriculum and teachers are the key resources which children utilise while further constructing their identity. The school curriculum should incorporate these as much as possible to provide children with a broad learning experience in which they can develop their sense of a shared and independent sense of communal identity. Curriculum subjects should be utilised to promote communal identity as much as possible, some suggestions have been listed below.

HISTORY

Exposure to the past and past experiences is vital in the formation of identity. Dixon and Hales (2014) call for a reconceptualisation of the curriculum, with a refined focus on local history, stating that it should encompass the community and people at its centre – increasing the relevance of today's diverse cultural society. History as a subject is inherently about people and places. History develops a sense of community diversity by bringing together people through a shared memory of the past which they themselves have not experienced. It is pivotal in an individual's understanding of how their local area came to be, creating an opportunity for identity construction.

History feeds on intrigue and engagement, building a sense of value towards others when the curriculum is built upon inclusivity. Providing a non-inclusive curriculum will lead to some children feeling disadvantaged or undervalued. When developing a history curriculum, children should be at the forefront; acknowledging the child's locality and the historical events of the area should be pivotal to the development of local identity. Notably, it should be perceived that local history is not limited to the immediate geographical area, but rather could make considerations to wider culture and heritage. In recent years, the local history curriculum has evolved to focus on the people and community rather than the physicality of an area (Tosh, 2015). Despite local history being present in the national curriculum since 1988, it has been taught in isolation; it should be embedded into the history curriculum. The current national curriculum (DfE, 2014) includes statutory guidance of local history units in both Key Stage 1 and 2, with a refined focus on significant local events, people and places.

RELIGIOUS EDUCATION (RE)

RE plays a pivotal role in developing children's understanding of different cultures and beliefs, an integral component to a child's development and growth. The exploration of diverse beliefs aims to decrease ignorance from an early age, which will allow children from diverse backgrounds to develop a sense of belonging and value – especially if their religion and/or beliefs have been acknowledged and engaged with in school. Ensuring opportunities for children to display their personal religious beliefs and practices contributes towards developing a communal identity of acceptance and understanding. This will be explored further in Chapter 7 on personal identity.

PERSONAL, SOCIAL, HEALTH AND ECONOMIC EDUCATION (PSHE)

PSHE is a safe space for children to explore different topics and develop their understanding further. While it is a non-statutory subject, it has remained this way to provide teachers with flexibility to determine the needs of their pupils and address them through appropriate high-quality lessons that equip them for adulthood (DfE, 2021). The British Red Cross website (www.redcross.org.uk/) has a library of teaching resources, some with a focus on identity and belonging, that challenges children to think critically of the stigma surrounding migration (for example), and what makes us who we are. One of the lesson resource packs explores refugees and immigrants in an attempt to encourage learners to think about why migrations happen and how they can make these people feel welcome. Teaching children about refugees in an approachable manner will help increase a child's tolerance and overall understanding of some contributing factors, which in turn increases a feeling of value towards refugees that children can embrace throughout their school and communities.

GEOGRAPHY

Geography has always been considered to have an important role in the lives of individuals, as our lives are shaped by geography in many ways. Many factors such as relationships, professions, nutrition and activities have been influenced by geography; it influences our identity. Individuals develop their identity according to the geographical region that they live in. A human's view of life, values and expectations is influenced by geographical contexts. Geography adds to communal identity through a shared common sense of memory due to living in the same geographical region. The feeling of belonging in a place that you live in relates to the definition of place, adding a sense of connection to people and place, shaping your communal identity. This is reiterated in the national curriculum which states that geography curriculum should develop a child's sense of place.

Place identity is a prominent concept of environmental psychology. It promotes that identities form due to the environments that we are exposed to. Place identity helps construct an individual's sense of communal identity as it consists of knowledge and emotions associated with experiences of a physical place. Place attachment underpins place identity, as it is the way in which an individual connects to a place, consequently developing their communal identity. These two concepts conjoined lay the framework of understanding where and why people feel at home or feel a sense of displacement. Essentially, where we grow up and live has a profound effect on our identity; however, we should be mindful of categorising others based on their sense of place.

REFLECTION 6.3

Think about your school curriculum.

Do you feel your school has used the flexibility in the national curriculum to develop a child's sense of communal identity?

Do the additional changes in your already-implemented curriculum instil a deeper sense of tolerance and understanding about identity formation?

PROMOTING CULTURAL ENGAGEMENT IN YOUR SCHOOL

In present-day schools there is a vast range of communal identities, representing both in and outside school. There are numerous whole-school strategies and event suggestions which could be implemented in school to help establish a positive communal identity. These will be discussed throughout this section of the chapter.

SCHOOL OF SANCTUARY

Schools are at the forefront of welcoming and supporting those who are forcibly displaced. The percentage of asylum seekers in the UK is on the increase, with nearly a quarter of those recorded in 2019 being under the age of 18 (Refugee Council, 2024). Therefore, it is pivotal for schools to be viewed as *schools of sanctuary*, meaning holding a recognition of the need to prepare for the arrival of prospective students seeking sanctuary.

The City of Sanctuary UK supports, develops and coordinates networks of welcome for asylum seekers. These networks range from community groups to councils, schools and universities working to develop inclusivity and compassion for individuals from a forced and displaced background. Furthermore, they organise the running of events, activities and initiatives across the UK promoting values in:

- *inclusivity*: welcoming people from all backgrounds, indicating a priority on diversity and equality;

- *openness*: encouraging collaborative work;

- *participation*: actively involving the people seeking sanctuary in decision-making;

- *inspire*: promoting enthusiasm and positivity;

- *integrity*: acting with the best interests of others in mind.

The City of Sanctuary UK website (https://cityofsanctuary.org/) provides resources for schools to develop as schools of sanctuary. The organisation encourages schools to become a place of welcome; educate on forced displacement; acknowledge the benefits of the new arrivals; and support children from a range of backgrounds to feel included and supported. In 1990 Nelson Mandela said (in a speech at Madison Park High School, Boston): 'Education is the most powerful weapon which you can use to change the world.' This is one of the driving quotes of this school initiative.

The City of Sanctuary began with the vision of the UK endeavouring to become a welcoming safe space for all; it uses its close partnerships with all the major refugee organisations to advocate for building a strong support system for people absconding due to violence and persecution across the world.

ANNUAL REFUGEE WEEK

Refugee Week takes place annually in June. A main teaching focus underpinning this week may help children develop an understanding of the vocabulary and issues surrounding refugees as discussed on the news, deepening their ability to celebrate the diversity and sense of inclusion in their school community. Refugee Week is a UK-wide celebration, acknowledging the contribution, creativity and resilience of refugees and people seeking sanctuary in the UK and across the globe. The National Literacy Trust website (https://literacytrust. org.uk/) provides plentiful resources to help prepare for this week of celebration, with a refined focus for the week – for example, the 2024 campaign is centred around the theme of Our Home. There are virtual author events and supporting classroom resources spanning across Early Years, Key Stage 1, Key Stage 2 and Key Stage 3 age groups. The website includes suggestions for implementation in schools and local communities, encouraging people to stand with refugees and develop early connections. Engaging with Refugee Week allows children to contribute to a large movement of people, gaining small initiatives to help develop bigger changes.

WORLD DAY FOR CULTURAL DIVERSITY FOR DIALOGUE AND DEVELOPMENT

This is a global event led by UNESCO, widely supported by the United Nations; it might more commonly be referred to simply as World Day for Cultural Diversity. It is a day dedicated to allowing people to reflect on diverse culture and cultural heritage. Every year it is celebrated on the 21st May; however, it can be acknowledged earlier if it doesn't fall on a school day. The event was set up to tackle various issues such as: recognising how culture diversity enriches society economically, intellectually and emotionally; culture being key to social inclusion; making global development more attainable; and to promote human rights along with freedoms. One of the main aims of the World Day for Cultural Diversity for Dialogue and Development is to improve access to the cultural and creative industries for people from more diverse backgrounds and to recognise the importance of cultural industries in the development of the world. It is about recognising and understanding people's differences but celebrating the promotion of peace and tolerance.

You could get involved by:

- displaying diversity posters;

- making recipes from across the world;

- listening to music from different cultures;

- having a dress-up day to celebrate different cultures across the world;

- creating artwork which promotes different cultures and diverse artists;

- fundraising for a charity to help make a difference – for example, the Diversity Trust.

Teaching websites such as Twinkl (www.Twinkl.co.uk) have a range of teaching resources in an effort to promote inclusion and diversity.

PRIDE MONTH

Pride is celebrated annually in the month of June. It is dedicated to recognising the LGBTQ+ communities across the UK and the rest of the world. It provides an opportunity to show support for individuals who identify as LGBTQ+ alongside increasing overall awareness and understanding of these individuals' identities. Pride is a vital topic to be explored in schools; only approximately 58 per cent of LGBTQ+ pupils report feeling safe at school on a daily basis, compared to 73 per cent of non-LGBTQ+ pupils, as recorded on Stonewall's 2022 report (Kelley and De Santos, 2022).

The Gay Rights movement advocates to end discrimination against LGBTQ+ people across all areas of life. Although society has increased the level of acceptance, harassment and discrimination are still prevalent in daily life. It is important for children to be made aware of the issues that remain in the modern world in creating an inclusive school community. Children can be exposed to LGBTQ+ awareness through history, themed books and sharing real-life stories of individuals. By recognising and embracing LGBTQ+ children in schools, an atmosphere of acceptance, respect and understanding will be fostered.

BLACK HISTORY MONTH

In the UK, Black History Month takes place annually in October. It is celebrated across the world, but originates from the USA. Black History Month allows for reflection over

6 Communal identity

the positive changes for the future; people acknowledge the contribution that black people have made to society, both historically and today. Each year a theme is selected by the US President for the event. The theme for 2024 was Black Health and Wellness, creating a spotlight on black medical professionals throughout history. Black History Month is important to celebrate the contributions to our community, building support for multiculturalism and diversity, while highlighting the inequalities that black people face. Making use of Black History Month in your school will create a welcoming and accepting atmosphere for children from other ethnicities.

ANTI-BULLYING WEEK

This initiative was developed by the Anti-Bullying Alliance to help raise awareness of the negative consequences of bullying, and to encourage people to rally against discrimination. The week has a main focus on celebrating inclusivity, respect and kindness. Each year there is a theme that your school may wish to adopt; the 2024 theme was Choose Respect. During Anti-Bullying Week, Odd Socks Day also takes place. Participants are encouraged to wear odd socks to express themselves and celebrate our unique identities. The Anti-Bullying Alliance has an abundance of school-aimed resources, making them accessible for schools to use to easily implement this inclusivity-developing week. Anti-Bullying Week is important to get involved with as it provides a vital opportunity to address intolerances towards diversity and differences between children, promoting tolerance for all.

RECOGNITION OF WORLD RELIGION CELEBRATIONS

In the UK, schools naturally recognise and teach about the Christian faith and partnering festival celebrations such as Christmas and Easter. This was because Christianity has previously been viewed as the majority religion being represented by children in primary schools. However, the percentage of ethnic minority children has increased over the previous year, with 37 per cent of pupils being recorded from a minority ethnic background in the 2023/24 school census (gov.uk, 2024). Due to this, the percentage of children representing different religions is on the increase, hence there is value in acknowledging and appreciating other religions and beliefs in school. This might be done through school celebrations of world religious festivals such as Diwali, Hanukkah, Lunar New Year and Ramadan. Table 6.2 gives the most common festivals of world religions and cultures, detailing how to show appreciation in school.

94

Table 6.2 World religious festivals

Celebration	Religion/culture	How to acknowledge in your school
Holi Festival of Colour	Hinduism	Decorate the classroom with the special colour of Holi, make and share sweet traditional treats
Dia De Los Muertos	Mexican	Encourage children to make or decorate an Ofrenda (built to honour and remember loved ones who have passed away)
Lunar New Year	Chinese	Make and decorate simple paper lanterns or traditional Chinese origami
Ramadan	Islam	Take time for mindfulness, encourage children to keep a Ramadan journal and reflect on their thoughts and feelings
Easter	Christianity	Reflect over the Easter story and make corresponding craft
Christmas	Christianity	Read the Christmas story and re-enact as a nativity story
Diwali	Hinduism and Sikhism	Teach the story of Rama and Sita, and the Sikh story of Guru Hargobind's fight against injustice make Diwali lights and practise a traditional Diwali dance
Hanukkah	Jewish	Play traditional games such as dreidel. Build a paper plate Menorah (a seven-branched candelabrum that is used in Jewish religious rituals)

BBC *Assemblies* for both Key Stage 1 and 2 provide age-appropriate resources, such as videos, questions, frameworks, songs, links and PowerPoints, to introduce children to some festivals of world religions. Twinkl has an abundance of similar-style materials which could be easily implemented to help raise awareness.

REFLECTION 6.4

Reflect on the cultural engagement strategies discussed above.

Do you think your school provides sufficient cultural engagement strategies to educate your children fully?

Think about some practical ways in which you could incorporate some of the suggested strategies in your school curriculum or events calendar.

CONCLUSION

This chapter has highlighted numerous initiatives that can be implemented in your school to celebrate diversity and make all children feel welcomed and appreciated throughout the school year. It is important to recognise and appreciate the variety of children's backgrounds as they make the school community brighter and well rounded overall.

By now you should have realised that identity is a complex concept with many contributing factors. This notion of identity will be further broken down, specifically examining what personal identity entails, in Chapter 7. It will build upon what has already been examined and will also discuss marginalised identities such as refugees, people with disabilities, people of colour, to name a few.

CHAPTER SUMMARY

Within this chapter we have considered:

- becoming familiar with recent publications that explore the concepts of identity and in-group/out-group;
- evidence that supports the argument that schools can take positive steps to enhance cultural engagement, bringing together a variety of personal identities among pupils and staff to inform a communal identity which promotes a sense of belongingness.

FURTHER READING

Identity, inclusion and child-centred education

www.claramariafiorentini.com/identity-inclusion-and-child-centred-ed

This website link provides suggestions to implement in your classroom while working in a diverse multicultural school to help promote a sense of belonging. It focuses on the notion that child-centred education and inclusion are interlinked and should be used in harmony.

Identity, society and equality lesson plans

www.mentallyhealthyschools.org.uk/resources/identity-society-and-equality-lesson-plans/
The Mentally Healthy School website has an array of resources to help teachers prepare lessons on identity and equality. It covers different key stages, depending on ability and overall understanding of the concepts. The resources available include a range of topics such as celebrating difference, stereotypes and discrimination.

BBC Teach *Primary School Assemblies: Festivals of World Religions*
www.bbc.co.uk/teach/school-radio/articles/z96xwnb#zqc3khv

The BBC Teach website provides a range of materials to take assemblies based on the common festivals of world religions. It provides resources for both key stages present in primary school, along with a timeline of when each festival takes place during the calendar year.

Bindu's Bindis by Supriya Kelkar

This children's book is a warm picture book about the bond between a grandmother and granddaughter, through their love for bindis and the culture that they share. It highlights the impact of xenophobia and prejudice and reinforces cultural pride for kids who may be hesitant to display the culture that ties them to their loved ones.

Can I Join Your Club? by John Kelly

A heart-warming children's book which celebrates the importance of diversity and friendship. Duck has started a club where there's one rule – everyone is welcome! This is reiterated because, when making friends, being yourself is all that counts.

7
PERSONAL IDENTITY
AMY BOYD AND KIERAN ROPER

THIS CHAPTER

The chapter will provide opportunities for readers to reflect upon:

- breaking down the facets of identity formation
- challenges faced by teachers and learners relating to marginalised identities
- curriculum areas which might lend themselves to promoting personal identity.

DEFINITIONS

- *Personal identity*: this refers to the characteristics to which you feel a special sense of attachment or ownership. It is the properties that define you as a person, and who you think you are.

INTRODUCTION

The previous chapter explored specifically communal identity. This chapter builds upon the previous, exploring identity at a personal level, and the characteristics which contribute towards its formation. Despite legislation like the Equality Act (2010), there often remains a disconnect between learners' personal identity and their school community, particularly if a learner is from a traditionally marginalised group (e.g. has a protected characteristic as defined in the Equality Act). This chapter specifically considers active steps that may be taken to engage students from diverse backgrounds and members of LGBTQ+ communities. These include introducing children to significant historical figures – for example, Alan Turing, Marie Curie, Oscar Wilde and Rosa Parks – who faced intense discrimination in society during their times. Children can also learn about classic and contemporary music – for example, Tchaikovsky, in order to understand the emotional tone of his music and evaluate his 19th-century compositions to develop an understanding of music history (DfE, 2013); discussions can be had about his life and what discrimination he faced despite his growing popularity.

WHAT IS THE EQUALITY ACT (2010)?

The Equality Act (DfE, 2010) proposed nine protected characteristics which include both gender reassignment and sex. With this, the failure to protect and provide quality education for LGBTQ+ pupils in schools was made illegal in order to create positive relationships with high levels of tolerance and respect. Importantly, there is no hierarchical structure between these protected characteristics; they are equal.

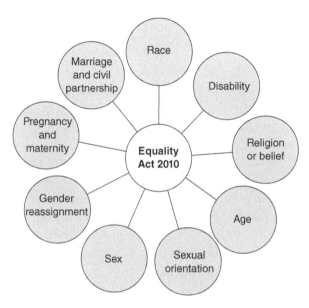

Figure 7.1 The nine protected characteristics of the Equality Act, 2010

WHAT IS IDENTITY?

Identity is an intriguing, yet rich concept to emerge from education. It plays a key role in all educational disciplines such as mathematics, biology and psychology (Splitter, 2007) and remains a pivotal conception in contemporary academic discourse. Our identity refers to the qualities, traits and characteristics that define who we are. In the education sector, this research has focused on identity construction of location, gender, sexual, social class and ethnicity. Each of these considerations shape the individual child into who they are and become.

Identity can be referred to in two forms:

1. *socialisation category*, defined by membership characteristics, attributes and rules which display expected behaviours, or
2. a *socially distinguishing feature* that an individual prides themselves by, viewing it as unchangeable but a consequence of sociality.

An individual can form identity through either separately or merged together. Through a socio-cultural theory (SCT) perspective (Fearon, 1999), identity can be socially formed, alongside human influences. These identities portray specific particularities which are sometimes contradictory and constantly evolving. Understanding the development of identity during school is an important task to be addressed, including institutional identity. Classrooms should provide a space of facilitation where children can explore and share who they are with their peers.

PERSONAL IDENTITY

Personal identity focuses on the question 'Who am I?' Unlike communal identity (Chapter 6), it is defined through an individual's beliefs, values, characteristics and behavioural styles with the meshing of cultural influences, as discussed in the section above. Personal identity is used to describe how individuals perceive themselves as unique and different. A range of research has indicated a strong personal identity is pivotal for psychological well-being and self-understanding. It is important to acknowledge that self and identity processes are not separate entities that exist in isolation; these processes may both enhance and limit the learning and engagement in classrooms. Schools should aim to encourage an outlook of a positive sense of self, empowering children with knowledge of their self and understanding of how they have developed. An individual's identities are unique to them; however, over time, groups of identities have fallen into a bracket known as *marginalised*. Marginalised identities will be explored later in the chapter.

ASPECTS OF IDENTITY

There are numerous aspects that construct the formation of identity, each of these have equal importance. We will look at these aspects of identity in detail (protected characteristics being identifiable by an *).

ABILITY AND DISABILITY*

Ability refers to an individual's competence to perform well at something, whereas disability refers to the challenges or limitations that an individual may face when completing tasks. An example of this is a professional footballer, who is extremely proficient at playing football; an individual in a wheelchair will not be as capable of playing the same sport without adaptations.

Able-bodied individuals, on the one hand, fail to recognise this aspect to be a contribution to their personal identity as it is often taken for granted. On the other hand, individuals with disabilities, either physical or mental – for example, autistic, D/deaf or amputees – may find their disability to be significant and/or life-changing and therefore view it as a central characteristic of their identity. It is essential that disability does not solely define the children by ensuring pupils of all abilities are respected and valued in the classroom, fostering an atmosphere of belongingness while attending school.

Schools have a responsibility to provide for children with disabilities, helping them to fulfil their full potential. Schools should endeavour to provide reasonable adjustments which may help level the playing field, minimising the individual's disadvantage against their peers. These reasonable adjustments include using organisations and people services, as schools are under a legal requirement according to the Equality Act. Suggestions to combat possible disability exclusion were discussed in Chapter 4.

AGE*

Age is a core social identity, as individuals belong to social groups according to their age. Generation X, Millennials, Generation Z and Alpha are the most common generations which individuals are associated with. Age groups may also refer to classifications of baby, toddler, children, teenager and, finally, adults. Notably, people's perception of age changes as they get older, as your role in your family or community shifts. This shift in position leads to a changing of understanding of how you view yourself and how you identify. Teachers therefore need to understand that generational differences can mean pupils have different outlooks, priorities and needs to themselves, while also being mindful that a difficult period which may seem very short to an adult can be perceived as much longer for a child.

CITIZENSHIP AND NATIONALITY

For hundreds of years, nationality and citizenship has helped form the sense of self. It is understood that nationality is a group of individuals that feel a sense of common identity and shared experiences, yet they are strangers to each other. In many countries, nationality is not a complete marker of identity apart from while travelling, when your nationality becomes the dominant identity marker of self.

Citizenship and nationality are unlikely to play a key role in identity construction in primary school, but it is vital to acknowledge and appreciate those children who view their identity with a heavy weighting on this aspect. It is likely that this will be true for new arrivals to the UK, particularly refugees and asylum seekers. Schools should encourage and promote discussions about the diverse citizenships and nationalities that are present in the school, creating an openness to developing further diversity tolerance.

ETHNICITY

Ethnicity refers to belonging to a group made up of people with a shared common cultural background or ancestry. Examples of ethnicities include, British-Asian, African American,

Latino, Cajun. Ethnicity is viewed as a cultural marker that showcases cultural features such as traditional rituals, beliefs, values, slang, religions, dances and accents. In some cases, ethnicity and race may have an overlap, but most of the time they are distinct entities – as one race might have multiple different ethnicities. For example, Roma and Irish are two different ethnicities, yet they are both Caucasian. However, in some instances, for children who have parents of different ethnic backgrounds their personal identity may carry multiple ethnicities, creating a multiethnic child.

The percentage of pupils from minority ethnic backgrounds across all primary schools in the UK is 37.4 per cent (gov.uk, 2024b), but this number is expected to rise in the coming years. Due to this increase, it is pivotal that schools are equipped to interact with diverse ethnicities and encourage a sense of inclusivity. This could be illustrated through the use of books from different cultures and backgrounds, celebrating diverse role models, celebrating pupils' heritage and being proactive about language use. More in-depth cultural engagement strategies were explored in Chapter 6.

FAMILY

An individual's sense of self is often connected with family and identity as a sibling, mum, dad, daughter, son and so on. In addition to this, parents indirectly teach and socialise their children through example. Children continuously observe their parents' interactions, choice-making and determinations between right and wrong which in turn impacts how a child's moral self is developed. We learn instrumental behavioural strategies such as the way we interact with the world and others. Family relationships are pivotal in a child's developing sense of belonging, which is related to their close and supportive relationships with family members. Family relations might not play an important role in the classroom, but teachers should understand a child's family dynamic and how it has helped construct a child's identity.

This includes having an awareness of *looked-after children*, a child who has been in the care of the local authority for more than 24 hours. These children may also be referred to as *children in care*. The percentage of these children has vastly increased over the last decade, with thousands of children being classified as looked after. It is important to recognise that many of these children have experienced forms of trauma such as abuse or neglect, so the notion of family may not have a positive effect on their identity.

GENDER REASSIGNMENT*

Gender is the self-identified reference to the characteristics of a woman, man, girl or boy, which have been socially constructed. Due to the social construction, gender varies between societies and is likely to evolve over time.

At birth your gender is ascribed according to your biological sex. In western societies, gender was traditionally viewed as a binary of male and female. However, over time this has become a spectrum, numerous variations of gender identifications have emerged with over

70 being recorded across the world (Allarakha, 2024) – such as *genderfluid*, an individual who does not adhere to one fixed gender but may identify with many. Another example is *agender*, a person who does not identify or experience any gender.

Gender-neutral toilets have been a major discourse in the education sector; this issue is prevalent in primary schools. More and more schools are installing gender-neutral toilets in the hope of becoming a more inclusive and supportive environment. Prior to the 2024 UK general election the Government (gov.uk, 2024a) announced new regulations intended to ensure that new buildings were to provide separate single-sex toilets for men and women along with self-contained universal toilets, depending on space allowance. However, schools were to be exempt from this initiative, therefore gender-neutral toilets would be at the school's discretion.

Gender has a profound influence on an individual's sense of self and identity; however, it is constantly evolving, therefore it is difficult to assert how gender may affect each individual child's identity formation. Teachers should endeavour to use the DfE's guidance (2020) on how to incorporate gender identity teaching in an appropriate, supportive and inclusive manner.

HOBBIES

While hobbies are not one of the protected characteristics under the Equality Act, they are instrumental to the construction of identity. Naturally, individuals affiliate with others who have a shared commonality. Hobbies can be viewed as a social identity because of the social interaction aspect which plays a part. Examples of hobbies may include playing sports, cooking, mathematics, reading, hiking, playing piano … the list is endless. In each classroom there will be a range of hobbies enjoyed by the children; this should be celebrated and acknowledged, as each hobby is as important as another, regardless of if it is viewed as slightly obscure.

Schools may wish to provide opportunities for children to explore and display their hobbies throughout the year. This might be in the form of talent shows, sports days or just in daily school life. Children should feel that their contribution to their hobbies is valued and respected, therefore it is vital to provide opportunities for all children to showcase their hobby. Moreover, in doing so you will create a more positive and inclusive environment in school, where children feel safe to display their identity.

LANGUAGES SPOKEN

Language is central to the construction of our social identity as it impacts life choices and thought processes. It determines how we view ourselves and relate to others. Similarly, accent may further develop your identity as it will be distinguishable to others once you start speaking. For example, Geordie is considered to be one of the most unique accents as it is strong and striking. Two Geordies are more likely to revel in conversation due to similar uses of tone and slang words, which others may not comprehend. Bilingual speakers may feel their identity is enhanced as they are able to communicate with two separate culture groups.

PERSONALITY

Personality is one's collection of characteristics, internal behaviours, cognition and emotional patterns that comprise a person's life perceptions. This includes their traits, hobbies, values and abilities. Personalities can be separated into two main groups – introvert and extrovert – but it is important to note that personalities may vary depending on the social context. Personality is what makes you *you*; it is unique to the individual, making it crucial in the development of your identity. Children should be made aware that everyone has their own personality, while there might be some shared likeness, mostly they are different. This notion could be explored in more detail in PSHE.

PHYSICAL APPEARANCE

Understandably physical appearance remains a feature of your identity. It can lead to others and you thinking differently about yourself, in either a positive or negative light. Historically there have been different physical features which are believed to be attractive, but 'beauty standards' are constantly changing over time. Due to the beauty standards, children may label themselves as 'pretty', 'ugly', 'handsome', etc.; however, these labels have been socially constructed by society. Nevertheless, these labels may have an impact on an individual's sense of self and value. Social media and camera phones have led to an increased preoccupation with looks for some children, with many feeling pressured to conform to a certain 'look'. Teachers need to be mindful of this and be sensitive to its effects on some pupils' self-esteem.

POLITICAL VIEWS

Political views might not have a profound impact on a child's formation of identity, but they will inform your social identity perception as a teacher. Recently, the status of people's political views has risen in terms of their sense of self. They can impact one's sense of core values and develop a sense of community with people of similar political perspectives. People may feel a political affiliation due to candidates or may identify with a political cause. As teachers, it is important to recognise that some parents and carers may have extreme political views which can lead to tensions in school. Meanwhile, as mandatory Prevent training in all education settings indicates, teachers need to be mindful of children of all ages potentially becoming radicalised by extreme political views.

PROFESSION

Although, again, profession is irrelevant for primary-aged children, it is relevant for teachers to ascertain how personal identity is constructed. Profession or occupation is pivotal to the formation of your identity because it is what you do on a daily basis. In the contemporary world, people are more likely to change professions throughout their working lives as their identity shifts and evolves over time. Children and young people's identity may be partly shaped by their parents' professions, particularly if they impact on family life – for example, having a parent in the military who may be posted abroad for extended periods, or working for a company which requires frequently moving to different locations meaning children need to regularly change schools and be 'the new boy/girl'.

RACE*

As explored in Chapter 1, the categorisation of humans based on shared physical or social qualities within a given society is defined as race. It refers to the biological association with groups of humans with shared characteristics – for example, skin pigmentation or facial features. Other dimensions of race include a shared history, traditions and use of language. Common racial groups are Asian, white, Hispanic, black or African American. As race is a protected characteristic, schools are held accountable for ensuring inclusion of differing children. Each racial group has shared genetic characteristics, which often makes them easily identifiable and therefore more susceptible to discrimination. Incorporating discussions of different racial groups and celebrating everyone's differences will create an environment of welcome and acceptance.

RELIGION*

For many people, religion is central in the formation of their personal identity. This is due to the construction of personal values through religion and forms their conception of an afterlife. Religion traditionally was an important feature of society, but in recent years it has been in decline in the UK. While some children may experience a secular family life where religion has very little influence, for others their family life will be significantly shaped by religion.

It is compulsory for all state-funded schools in England to teach religious education (RE). Although it is not considered part of the national curriculum, it is an important subject that helps develop children's understanding of the world's religions.

SEX*

This was discussed in detail in Chapter 3. It is critical to assert that gender and sex have become increasingly disconnected as aspects of identity; they should be viewed as separate contributing entities. For example, an individual born as a male may wish to identify as a feminine gender. It remains that many people adhere to their biological sex and gender, but with an evolving society more gender types may appear in primary classrooms.

SOCIAL CLASS

The socio-economic status (SES) of an individual is known as their social class, alongside the transitions and subcultural practices of that shared social class. Common well-known social classes are as follows: working class, middle class and upper class. Social class plays a small, yet significant role in the construction of personal identity. For some people, self-defined social class is an important part of their identity. This is not always connected to their income. This notion of social class and its impact on educational attainment was explored in Chapter 2.

VALUES AND BELIEFS

Personal values and beliefs are a central aspect of your personal identity. For example, an individual may identify as a humanitarian, or as an individual which values honesty in all situations. Values and beliefs are often connected to other aspects of identity such as political or religious associations. For example, a child who has grown up with a low socio-economic status may value social justice highly and value hard work to create independence.

Notably, people's values and beliefs will evolve over time, depending on what their individual priorities are. Things you valued as a child in school might not hold the same importance to you as a class teacher. This is because your life experiences inform and change what you consider to be crucial about a person at any given time in your life.

SEXUAL ORIENTATION*

Sexual orientation is another protected characteristic which encompasses the type of people that you are romantically attracted to, including homosexual, heterosexual, bisexual or asexual relationships. This might not seem relevant to the primary classroom, but, with the fast-changing environment of the world, these concepts are more open from a younger age bracket, with some children identifying themselves while in primary schools. As of September 2020, all primary schools were required to teach about different families, including LGBTQ+ families, as part of relationships education (DfE, 2020). This change introduces primary-aged children to different sexual orientations and different relationship types in society.

This statutory educational requirement has raised some concern from parents; however, the DfE sees value in this early introduction in a drive to promote a sense of tolerance, acceptance and respect to help counter the increasing amount of homophobia that is present in the media. Schools should especially promote the change in attitudes towards homosexuality, as today it is widely accepted in western countries.

REFLECTION 7.1

Do you know if your school has any policies for the above protected characteristics? Check the school website or get in touch with the senior leadership or the designated school leader. If yes, explore some of them to see what provision looks like in practice. If not, think about how you can bring about positive change in your classroom to support learning and model how to respect, understand and accept individual differences among diverse groups.

MARGINALISED IDENTITIES

Although everyone's identities should be valued as equal there are some groups which remain marginalised, who still experience instances of mistreatment or discrimination by society. These include women, refugees, people with disabilities, people of colour, LGBTQ+, indigenous people and people classed as being of a low socio-economic status.

Many marginalised children feel a sense of fear when entering a new classroom and before deciding whether you and your classroom offer a safe space for them. This sense of fear or discomfort has developed either through personal experience and/or social construction of societal norms.

Let's focus on discrimination faced by women and LGBTQ+ communities in society in further detail. In its development from the Sex Discrimination Act of 1975 which covered areas like education, employment and advertisement, the Equality Act (2010) proposed protected characteristics (DfE, 2010) which aimed to 'tackle all forms of bullying, particularly homophobic and transphobic bullying' and of women by improving the 'lives of victims'. Although it is evident to some extent that the discrimination against women has decreased, a Women in Football survey showed that two-thirds of female footballers have experienced gender discrimination (Rasul, 2022). Moreover, many examples of LGBTQ+-related deaths have become apparent in recent years, including transwomen, such as Brianna Ghey. Most LGBTQ+ individuals have faced discrimination throughout their lives despite the policies implemented to reduce this. Distressingly, Barnes and Carlile (2018) found that the hate crime prevalence for women and LGTBQ+ communities in Britain has rocketed from 9 per cent to 78 per cent in recent years. Consequently, the effectiveness of policies like the Equality Act may be dubious and is certainly proven to be insufficient. Practitioners need to understand the historic discrimination against these groups and how best to support them and promote tolerance of these groups within the classroom.

The 2030 Agenda for Sustainable Development was adopted by United Nations member states in 2015, providing a blueprint for peace and prosperity for people and the planet. There are 17 Sustainable Development Goals (SDGs; see https://sdgs.un.org/goals) which are an urgent call for action by all countries in a global partnership. One of those SDGs (2030), Goal 5, is 'gender equality' where authorities must 'build and upgrade education facilities that are child ... and gender-sensitive' that enable effective learning environments which undertake the philosophies of safety and inclusivity. While the equality gap between men's and women's pay and job prospects has closed significantly, many faith schools are not prepared to deliver LGBTQ+ aspects of the Equality Act. This demonstrates that implementing such policies can still be a challenge despite the LGBTQ+ Equality Action Plan proposing to prohibit homophobic and transphobic bullying.

■ CASE STUDY 7.1

Promoting gender equality through picture books

A primary school in Manchester created an LGBTQ+-friendly environment where pupils feel safe by providing books that increase children's awareness of LGBTQ+ issues as they attempted to promote the 'acceptance of nonnormative gender presentations'. Following are some of picture books which the school provided in the classrooms to facilitate discussion among pupils:

Feminist Baby by Loryn Brantz

Boy, Can He Dance by Eileen Spinelli

Jacob's School Play: Starring He, She, and They by Ian and Sarah Hoffman

The Strangeworlds Travel Agency by L. D. Lapinski

Daddy, Papa and Me by Leslea Newman and Carol Thompson

Picture books support learning how to respect, understand and accept individual differences among diverse groups. Children often find it more meaningful to engage and relate to a character, mainly the protagonist, through picture books allowing them to understand that not all families are the same (for example, single-parent households and families with LGBTQ+ parents). However, it is important to bear in mind that it can be easy to marginalise these groups rather than affirm them. Hence, pedagogically, teachers should intentionally invest in a gender balance of books that alter heteronormative views. Significantly, over the years, picture books have shown fewer obvious gender stereotypes; however, subtle stereotypes may still exist.

REFLECTION 7.2

Reflect upon the provision in your school and think about ways in which you could make positive, more inclusive changes.

Do you use picture books in your classroom? Consider the books you use.

Do they reflect diversity?

Do they model how to respect, understand and accept individual differences among diverse groups?

HOW DO TEACHERS' ATTITUDES AND CONFIDENCE INFLUENCE THE PROMOTION OF LGTBQ+ GROUPS?

Silveira and Goff (2016) examined the attitudes of 75 in-service and 105 pre-service Australian teachers towards trans students. They reported participants having more positive transgender attitudes which correlated with teachers' confidence in supporting trans students. Another study (Page, 2017) found that younger teachers had high levels of comfort in using LGBTQ+ texts and were willing to implement these philosophies. Caution must be observed as this Australian study creates a generalisation that a *'generational shift will remedy the problem* of excluding LGBTQ+ content' (n.p., emphasis in original). However, teachers with *cultural competence* should address and promote cultural diversity in their classroom, particularly in relation to gender and sexuality. Overall, the above-mentioned research advocates how the use of training may increase teacher confidence and competence in supporting women and LGBTQ+ pupils.

We conclude this section by providing an exemplar medium-term plan for teachers to use or adapt for their own teaching in their primary classrooms.

Table 7.1   Exemplar planning: Summer Term 2 medium-term plan for celebrating 'Gender and Sexuality' in the foundation subjects

Week 1	
Lesson	Exploring the similarities and differences between the discrimination of women and LGBTQ+ people throughout history (History).
Learning objective	<ul><li>I can contribute to a discussion of the similarities and differences about the discrimination of all women and LGBTQ+ people in different societies.</li><li>I can gather and use information about forms of discrimination against people in societies and consider the impact this has on people's lives.</li><li>I can discuss issues of the diversity of cultures values and customs in our society.</li></ul>

(Continued)

7 Personal identity

Table 7.1   (Continued)

Activities/ teaching sequence	**Starter**
	Begin by listening to 'Dear Future Husband' by Meghan Trainor and talk about what children think the song means.
	Who is it talking about? Does it link to anything pupils know about history linked with the oppression of women and how many couldn't work?
	Activity
	In this session, the class will explore the jobs, income, clothes, opinions and songs about women vs men throughout time.
	This will link to their current history topic (whether that be Victorian medieval etc.).
	Teacher to provide information about the historical context of power and privilege in relation to gender.
	• Show that current gender roles are not rigid; that they have changed over time and that making change is possible (show video).
	• Consider collective power and how power can be used positively to challenge misuse of power. Have a debate about the similarities and differences about the discrimination of women and LGBTQ+ people in different societies.
	Main task
	Using picture prompts from the debate in the lesson to create a comparative poster which shows the differences throughout time of the discrimination of certain elements of society (women and LGBTQ+).
	Plenary
	Discuss the values within today's society.
	Are people more accepted in today's society than in the 19th or 20th centuries?
Resources	• Music from the playlist.
	• History of women's rights video.
	• A PowerPoint presentation for the class teacher to use, made by the teacher.
	• Picture prompts for poster about the differences of women in society (including jobs, clothes, etc.).
	• Short articles about the oppression of women and LGBTQ+ communities.
Assessment	• Are they able to create a poster about the similarities and differences surrounding the discrimination of women and LGBTQ+ communities in different societies and time periods?
	• Are they able to value others as equals and understand we're all unique?
	• Are they able to compare the rights of these groups in different cultures?

Week 1	
Link to national curriculum	• Understand historical concepts such as similarity, difference and significance, and use them to draw connections, draw contrasts, analyse trends. • Show tolerance of and respect for the rights of others.
Week 2	
Lesson	Exploring historical figures in history that made a difference to their discriminated community (History/Science).
Learning objective	• I know about the lives of significant individuals in the past such as Rosa Parks, Oscar Wilde, Alan Turing and Marie Curie. • I can describe how these figures made a difference in modern-day society.
Activities/ teaching sequence	**Starter** Begin by listening to 'Superwoman' by Alicia Keys and talk about what children think the song means. Who is it talking about? Does it link to anything they know about history? Then get the class to recall things they learnt last week about the oppression of discriminated groups throughout history (create mind maps on board). **Activity** In this session the children will explore and find historical facts about four different historical figures which were either important women or represented a discriminated group. These include Wilde, Turing, Parks and Curie. Each group will be given someone to research further after going through each of them as a class. Their job is to create a fact file about their chosen historical figure.
Resources	• Music from the Spotify playlist. • Marie Curie video. • Marie Curie facts. • PowerPoint and videos made by staff to talk about all of these people. • Copies of Wilde poetry.
Assessment	• Are they able to describe how these historical figures were discriminated against and how they can teach us to value all types of people? • Can they describe who these people are?
Link to national curriculum	• Know about the lives of significant individuals in the past. • Show tolerance of and respect for the rights of others.
Week 3	
Lesson	Read picture books which will tell the class a story about the oppression of gay/queer people in order to develop tolerance of all (PSHE/English/Art).

(Continued)

7 Personal identity

Table 7.1   (Continued)

Learning objective	• I can describe the challenges faced by many discriminated groups, such as LGBTQ+. • I can understand the importance of showing tolerance of and respect for the rights of others, including LGBTQ+ identifying communities. • I could write a speech from the perspective of a discriminated person to persuade people to be tolerant.
Activities/ teaching sequence	**Starter** Begin by listening to 'Champion' by RuPaul and talk about what the children think the song means. Who is RuPaul and what does she/he do? How successful have they been and what does this show you about today's society? **Activity** Pupils will read themed stories about the challenges faced by LGBTQ+ communities to heighten the visibility of these groups. Write a speech from the perspective of a discriminated person to persuade their crowd to be tolerant. **Plenary** Discuss the importance of tolerance of different people and how all people are unique.
Resources	• LGBTQ+-themed books and picture books such as *Daddy, Papa and Me* and *The Strangeworlds Travel Agency*. • Music from the Spotify playlist. • Examples of empowering speeches such as Martin Luther King and Malala Yousafzai.
Assessment	• Are pupils able to understand why expressing who they are is important and that not everyone is the same? • Are they able to think from a different perspective and write a persuasive speech?
Link to national curriculum	• To create sketchbooks to record their observations and use them to review and revisit ideas. • Make inferences on the basis of what is being said, done or observed. • Show tolerance of and respect for the rights of others.
Week 4	
Lesson	Explore music by Tchaikovsky and look at the history around his homosexuality and how people perceived him (Music/History).
Learning objective	• I can listen to, review and evaluate music across a range of historical periods and genres (Tchaikovsky). • I know about the lives of significant individuals in the past such as Tchaikovsky.

7 Personal identity

Week 4	
Activities/ teaching sequence	**Starter** Begin by recalling facts about Oscar Wilde. Think about who he was? Why was he imprisoned? What happened to him in his life? Discuss as a class. **Activity** The session will be focusing on the historical discrimination of Tchaikovsky and listening to some of his music. Talk about how he was homosexual and how he was, historically, associated with social prejudice which resulted in the myth of him as neurotic, lonely and disturbed. Compare this to him now: is he more respected now? Why might this be the case? What developments have occurred through history? Listen to some of Tchaikovsky's songs and evaluate his music; have pupils heard his music before and do they like it? Then write a letter to the government persuading them to celebrate LGBTQ+ communities throughout England; present some to class.
Resources	• Tchaikovsky music from the Spotify list. • PowerPoint and videos made by staff to talk about Tchaikovsky. • Copies of Wilde's poetry. • Fact sheets about Wilde and Tchaikovsky.
Assessment	• Are they able to recall facts about Tchaikovsky and his life as a homosexual composer? • Can they compare how people have gained respect for these historical figures through their contribution to their field?
Link to national curriculum	• Listen to, review and evaluate music across a range of historical periods and genres. • Know about the lives of significant individuals in the past.
Week 5	
Lesson	Allow the children to express themselves through dance (PE/PSHE/Music).
Learning objective	• I can express myself through dance and music. • I can understand the importance of showing tolerance of and respect for the rights of others. • I can understand the importance of expressing myself and my identity.
Activities/ teaching sequence	**Starter** Read *Giraffes Can't Dance* and discuss some of the different dances that are mentioned in the text. Watch some age-appropriate dance moves online.

(Continued)

7 Personal identity

Table 7.1 (Continued)

Week 5	
	Activity
	Play some music for the children to dance to.
	Allow time for children to express themselves creatively and perform their own dances, drawing some of the moves from the book and the clips.
	Use the speaking and listening opportunity for children to express which dance they like and why.
	Write a short description about which song they enjoyed the most and why.
	Plenary
	Revisit the theme of the book – sometimes when you are different you just need a different song.
	What does this mean? Ask children about a time they wanted to do something different or felt different.
Resources	• *Giraffes Can't Dance*, storybook.
	• Online dance clips (age-appropriate).
	• Music from the Spotify playlist.
Assessment	• Are the children able to express how they are feeling through dance?
	• Can they explain what their thought processes were when creating the dance?
	• Can they infer what is implied in *Giraffes Can't Dance*?
Link to national curriculum	• Perform dances using a range of movement patterns.
	• Tolerance of and respect for the rights of others.
	• Read a book with high fluency.
Week 6	
Lesson	Focus on researching a historical figure who experienced oppression (give examples for the children to research) (ICT/History).
Learning objective	• I can know about the lives of significant individuals in the past.
	• I can understand the importance of showing tolerance of and respect for the rights of others including LGBTQ+-identifying communities.
Activities/ teaching sequence	**Starter**
	Begin by listening to 'King of My Heart' by Taylor Swift and talk about what the children think the song means.
	Who is it talking about? Does it link to anything they know about history?
	Think about what significance this song has.
	Activity
	This session will predominantly be student-led research as we want them to explore the historical/modern-day figures that have either experienced or imposed oppression due to their sexuality or gender and create a fact file on them.

114

	They should also explain why promoting tolerance of every person is respectful and something which we all should do. The people they can research: • Mary Somerville (1780-1872) • Barbara McClintock (1902-1992) • RuPaul (1960-present) • Divina de Campo (1983-present) • Leslie Feinberg (1949-2014) • Marcel Proust (1871-1922) • Margaret Thatcher (1925-2013) • Marguerite Antonia Radyclyffe Hall (1880-1943) • Virginia Woolf (1882-1941)
Resources	• Music from the Spotify playlist. • History of women's rights video. • PowerPoint presentation for the class teacher to use. • Access to a computer suite for children to research.
Assessment	• Are they able to interpret what the meaning of a song is and apply this to the promotion of gender and sexuality? • Are they able to research someone who has faced or imposed oppression onto discriminated groups?
Link to national curriculum	• Tolerance of and respect for the rights of others. • To search technologies effectively, appreciate how results are selected and ranked.

The principles outlined here for celebrating gender and sexuality and creating a more inclusive classroom can be adapted to all the aspects of identity discussed earlier in this chapter.

REFLECTION 7.3

Choose another of the aspects of identity discussed earlier in the chapter and try to design Week 1 of an exemplar for it.

What are the key lessons? Is there overlap with the Gender and Sexuality lessons listed here? What are some differences?

What resources will you need?

SO, WHAT MORE CAN TEACHERS DO?

Being kind to children from marginalised backgrounds is not enough. Marginalised children deserve teachers who actively acknowledge and value their identity in the classroom, nurturing a child's belongingness. Teachers should adhere to the Equality Act (2010) which provides a consolidated source of discrimination law, alongside any school-implemented policies such as Accessibility, Anti-bullying, British values and SEN. It is crucial to note that how teachers regard individual children has an impact on the quality of that child's educational life, both socially and academically. Below are suggestions which can be easily implemented in your classroom.

CLASSROOM VISUALS

Hanging imagery and supportive messages around the classroom walls helps with the impression your classroom environment generates. Posters which affirm children's identities in a supportive manner will send the message that this classroom is accepting and welcoming to all. Simply ask yourself whether each child can personally connect with something in your room and adjust as appropriate.

IMPLEMENTING SUPPORTIVE LANGUAGE

Words matter to children; the words you use or do not use play a critical role in supporting a child's identity. Words can equally affect all children, including those classed as marginalised – whether that be a teacher's comment or one of their peers'. By being aware of the language used and the groups forming in your classroom, you will help more children feel included. Teachers should endeavour to have a rounded understanding of the different cultures represented in the class and make use of correct terminology and language when appropriate.

CONSTRUCT A CULTURALLY DIVERSE CURRICULUM

As a teacher, it is your responsibility to ensure children's identities are valued and acknowledged all year long, and not reserved for identified months or weeks such as Pride Month or Refugee Week. Make use of the curriculum to help pupils view themselves in different subjects, enriching children's understanding of the diverse world around them. Subject-specific suggestions for developing identity were also discussed at the end of Chapter 6.

REMOVE EXISTING BARRIERS

Proactively ensuring your classroom is accessible and inclusive for those with disabilities can send a welcoming message to all the children. This might be allowing the classroom space to be open and free of clutter to help children with physical disabilities navigate the room at ease, or providing scaffolds for children who might struggle to complete tasks independently, allowing them to access the curriculum to the same extent as their peers.

REFLECTION 7.4

Choose one idea from the above list and think about how you can implement strategies within your school environment.

What are the barriers or challenges here? What can you do to overcome them?

What resources will you need?

CONCLUSION

Children's sense of personal identity can be developed through an array of strategies in the primary classroom as highlighted in this chapter. However, due to its vastness we have not been able to discuss all subjects of the curriculum. Instead, this chapter focused on providing examples of how teachers can be empowered to demonstrate and teach tolerance of and respect for the rights of others (particularly LGBTQ+ groups) through use of picture books and carefully chosen music, events and personalities from history – thereby providing children with the skills, knowledge and understanding they need to develop into well-rounded, informed and tolerant individuals.

CHAPTER SUMMARY

Within this chapter we have considered:

- how different characteristics have developed our sense of identity;
- some key policies that seek to support groups of learners being marginalised due to their identity (e.g. LGBTQ+);
- possible recommendations for practitioners to implement in schools and classrooms.

FURTHER READING

PSHE Association

https://pshe-association.org.uk

This website is the only national body for PSHE leads and teachers. It aims to improve PSHE lessons for all children, with an abundance of resources created by subject specialists to aid teaching.

Understanding, exploring and supporting children's identity development

www.researchinpractice.org.uk/media/0tkdn3ht/understanding-exploring-and-supporting-children-s-identity-development_pt_web.pdf

This accessible practice tool aims to support teachers in exploring the concept of identity with children. It breaks down identity further, exploring and reflecting on self-identity as a practitioner. This resource provides further examples of supporting a child's identity development.

An Introduction to Supporting LGBTQ+ Children and Young People

www.stonewall.org.uk/sites/default/files/final_-_an_intro_to_supporting_lgbt_young_people_-_april2022.pdf

This online PDF has been developed by Stonewall, a charity dedicated to the equity of all LGBTQ+ people. They have produced a helpful introductory guide to help practitioners with supporting children identifying as LGBTQ+, including information on recommendations on how to create an inclusive environment.

Identity and Belonging Resource Pack by British Red Cross

www.redcross.org.uk/get-involved/teaching-resources/identity-and-belonging

Here are some activities to encourage children and young people to think critically about stigma and migration, and what makes us who we are. By engaging with this resource pack, pupils will be able to consider multiple points of view and how they might be perceived by others; explore the impact of stigma; reflect on assumptions about migration; and, finally, recognise what makes us human.

Understanding identity

www.facinghistory.org/en-gb/resource-library/understanding-identity-0

In this lesson, students consider the question 'Who am I?' and identify social and cultural factors that shape identity by reading a short story and creating personal identity charts.

Personal identity wheel

https://sites.lsa.umich.edu/equitable-teaching/personal-identity-wheel/

The personal identity wheel is a worksheet activity that encourages pupils to reflect on how they identify outside social identifiers. The worksheet prompts students to list adjectives they would use to describe themselves, skills they have, favourite books, hobbies, etc. It is best used as an icebreaker activity to encourage students to reflect on the relationships and dissonances between their personal and communal identities.

It Feels Good to Be Yourself: A Book About Gender Identity by Theresa Thorn

This children's picture book introduces the concept of gender identity to the youngest reader. It is a sweet, yet straightforward exploration of gender identity which will give children a fuller understanding of themselves and others while discussing this important topic with sensitivity.

8
GLOBALISATION AND ENVIRONMENTAL DEPRIVATION

ROSIE LEGENDER, LUCY DAVIES AND KULWINDER MAUDE

THIS CHAPTER

The chapter will provide opportunities for readers to reflect upon:

- how places outside the UK are taught to children in the UK to enable them to engage with a globalised world

- how places (e.g. in the UK) have changed as a result of globalisation and migration

- how extremely high levels of both wealth and poverty (resources) exist in possibly the world's most diverse communities and yet they may be struggling with global problems ranging from the impact of climate change through to more local issues raised by the area's rapidly changing population

- how schools could play a part in reducing resulting inequalities

- the challenges faced by refugee children starting school in the UK.

DEFINITIONS

- *Refugee*: a person who has been forced to leave their country in order to escape war, violence, persecution or a natural disaster. They have crossed an international border to seek safety.

- *Asylum seeker*: a person who has left their home country and enters another country seeking protection from prosecution and serious human rights violations in another country. This individual has not yet been legally recognised as a refugee and is waiting to receive a decision on their asylum claim.

8 Globalisation and environmental deprivation

- *English as an additional language (EAL)*: this could be a second language or a third, fourth, etc.

- *Globalisation*: this refers to the integration of global economics, industries, markets, culture and policy-making around the world free from socio-political control; it reduces distances between regions/countries through a global network of trade, communication, immigration and transportation.

- *Critical cultural awareness*: a deep, nuanced, and complex understanding of diversity that includes the skill of effectively communicating across cultures.

- *Distant places*: these can be viewed in two ways – places that are far away geographically or have a distant connection to someone emotionally (this chapter refers to the former), also known as farplaces.

INTRODUCTION

Globalisation is the increasing integration and interdependence of countries' economies, societies, technology, cultures, politics and ecology. It has an impact on communities and poverty in the UK because of our many connections with other parts of the world; the relationship between economic and social trends; and our place in the global economy. The UK economy is integrated with other parts of the world and many people's economic well-being is tied to the global economy. Schools play a part in teaching children how the global economy influences poverty and inequality in the UK, and how far these trends can be managed. People on low incomes engage with the global economy as consumers, workers and users of services. To feel overlooked, misunderstood, or ignored, either as an individual or a group, impacts on our sense of self, of our intrinsic worth (Clair et al., 2012). Even more damaging can be the misrepresentation of peoples in the global community which perpetuate dangerous stereotypes and sense of *otherness*. This chapter encourages readers to incorporate critical and cultural awareness into their teaching to prepare children for an increasingly globalised world.

THE IMPACT OF GLOBALISATION ON THE UK

Globalisation has significantly transformed the UK, influencing its economy, culture and society. Economically, the UK has become deeply integrated into the global market, with increased trade, foreign investment and the proliferation of multinational corporations, leading to greater economic growth and diversity of goods and services. Culturally, globalisation has enriched the UK with a mosaic of cultures, cuisines and traditions, making it a more multicultural society. This cultural exchange has also influenced fashion, music and entertainment, creating a vibrant and dynamic society. Socially, globalisation has facilitated greater mobility and immigration, contributing to a more diverse population. However, it has also brought challenges, such as economic inequalities and cultural tensions, requiring policies to help the UK adapt seamlessly and also efforts to encourage social cohesion. Globalisation has reshaped the UK's identity, creating both opportunities and complexities as the UK has become more interconnected.

GLOBALISATION AND EDUCATION

Including globalisation into the school curriculum provides exciting opportunities to add an international dimension to children's learning experiences and introduce them to places that may encourage them to travel and continue to learn about various cultures over time. Despite this, the educational impacts of globalisation have been poorly understood, with the term often only associated with political-economic influence or technological advancements. Intense global changes have required increased international communication and understanding, significantly impacting educational reform. Unlike previous generations, 21st-century learners are regularly exposed to growing ethnic, cultural and linguistic diversity in the classroom. It has been widely acknowledged that students are now more aware of global issues and must appreciate the growing relationship between local and global dimensions. An individual's intercultural competence is significant in this process, as students must deal with growing heterogeneity in a globalised world. This notion describes the ability to interact effectively and appropriately in intercultural situations. In the 21st century, the skill of dealing *constructively* with a multitude of cultural values, attitudes and norms is a key factor in employment and social cohesion. Overall, it is necessary for individuals to adapt positively to our diverse and internationalised world.

The ability of geography to connect distant cultures to one's locality is further supported by Ofsted (2021) in its most recent geography review which explains that the subject has a general aim to appreciate diversity, build bridges and bring people together. This is particularly important in English education, where a third of school-aged students are from minority ethnic backgrounds.

FOSTERING AN UNDERSTANDING OF 'DISTANT PLACES'

Considering the significance of geography as a medium for exposing 'explanatory relationships' and making 'sense of the world and its people' (Ofsted, 2021, n.p.), it is important to discuss the current state of primary geography education and its relevance in the promotion of stereotypes. The English national curriculum (DfE, 2013, p. 1) follows a central theme of 'knowledge' and 'deep understanding' within geography. This includes: the recurring elements of interaction, context, similarity and contrast, particularly between a child's locality and a distant place. The term 'place' used here refers to both the physical and human

8 Globalisation and environmental deprivation

characteristics of a given location; the study of place can develop an understanding of how these characteristics 'interrelate and interact' with one another (*National Geographic*, 2022).

In Key Stage 1, children must compare a region in the UK to a 'contrasting' non-European country (DfE, 2013, p. 2); in Key Stage 2 they must compare a UK region to a European country and a region in North or South America. Thus, the distant place ranges widely, depending on the school's chosen contrasting location. This approach can provide educators with the flexibility needed to make learning relevant to their schools.

It is also possible, however, that these vague criteria create a distorted or unclear description of a distant place, posing questions regarding what makes a place 'distant', and by whom is this decided. The process assumes that any location outside Europe is a distant place, which is perhaps an over-generalisation and should be avoided in geography teaching. It is also interesting to note the use of vocabulary in the curriculum, such as 'contrasting' to describe distant places.

Although it is important for children to create links between cultures, focusing on them as *contrasting* places could be problematic. In doing so, the similarities between geographies can be disregarded and, often, children begin to develop an 'us and them' mentality. This issue is a longstanding one and, while it was damaging in previous decades, it is perhaps more so now as it leaves children unprepared for multicultural societies.

The discipline of geography has an issue of 'persistent and overwhelming whiteness' where white interests are normalised and constantly reinforced (Noxolo, 2017, p. 317). Instead, the geography national curriculum (DfE, 2013) should encourage learners to view distant places in *continuum and diversity*, not in terms of *difference and contrast*. This perception can be difficult for students to develop if geographical knowledge is presented to them in a closed-minded or oversimplified way.

CASE STUDY 8.1

Sam

Sam was teaching their first geography lesson as a first-year early career teacher (ECT). They had taught individual lessons of geography while a trainee teacher but had not planned, delivered and assessed a whole topic. As part of introducing the children to different continents Sam planned a lesson on Africa, starting with asking the children what they already knew about Africa. Several children said they had seen Africa on Comic Relief appeals; one said their uncle had been to South Africa on holiday. Overall, the children's prior knowledge was limited.

Sam showed the children a map of the world and located Africa, pointing out how far it was from the UK and that it was in the southern hemisphere. They then had a carousel of activities where children worked in groups, spending a few minutes at each table looking at and answering worksheets based on the following resources:

- pictures of various parts of Africa including the Valley of the Kings in Egypt;

- Serengeti National Park;

- real currency, the South African Rand which depict the big five (lion, leopard, elephant, buffalo and rhino) and fact sheets about each animal;

- travel brochures on safari holidays with worksheet questions about the type of activities available.

At the end of the lesson, Sam asked the children to write three things they had learnt about Africa from the lesson on Post-it notes so they could assess learning. Sam was disheartened to find many children had written things like:

- the 'big five' are animals that roam around Africa;

- Africa is made up of deserts and safari parks;

- the buildings in Africa are ancient;

- safari parks are where people in Africa go to have fun.

They realised that the resources they had used engaged the children, but had not provided a full picture of the continent. They also realised that many of the children were not mentioning any names of countries and just thinking of Africa as a homogeneous region.

REFLECTION 8.1

Where, in the above case, did Sam go wrong?

What could be done instead to address this so that misconceptions could be addressed by the end of the unit of work?

Who could Sam talk to for advice within their school?

CHALLENGES

There are two main challenges facing best practice in delivering high-quality lessons about distant places. Firstly, the current discipline of geography is a 'configuration around normalised white experiences' (Milner, 2020, p. 105). Not only has this significantly benefited white students within higher levels of geographical education – consequently contributing to the attainment gap observed in the subject between children from other ethnicities and white British pupils – it has also meant a lost opportunity to gain meaningful understanding of the wider world. Secondly, geography has often had a 'relatively low status' (Ofsted, 2021, n.p.) and there has been repeated criticism of the limited amount of good or excellent teaching, especially in primary schools.

Ofsted (2021) suggest poor teacher subject knowledge as a potential explanation for the poor state of geography education. Poor teacher subject knowledge has been an ongoing issue which Ofsted believe is, in part, the cause of 'superficial' or 'exotic' geography learning which could 'reinforce stereotypes' (Ofsted, 2011, p. 15). The stagnation in teachers' geography expertise, including both their knowledge and confidence, flags a cause for concern for the level of critical cultural awareness present within geography teaching in England. Overall, considering the crucial role of teacher knowledge in challenging the predominant stereotype, it is essential for all geography educators to uphold a high quality of critical cultural awareness.

STEREOTYPING

Stereotypes are images we create in our heads, encompassing oversimplified, negative and naive attitudes towards distant places. As one of the most important subjects in the development of international understanding, geography learning plays a significant role in the formation of stereotypical perceptions. The current low status and poor state of geography teaching in English primary schools (Ofsted, 2021) supports the proposal that *self and other* stereotypes are being encouraged. Such geographical stereotypes have overlooked the similarities and interconnectedness between local and global dimensions (DfES, 2005). Unfortunately, Ofsted (2021) recently found that almost half of schools do not teach the required knowledge included in the geography national curriculum (DfE, 2013), and observed many students learning with misconceptions, including the stereotypes mentioned above (Ofsted, 2011).

THE FORMATION OF STEREOTYPES

Stereotypes are not a new phenomenon. Said's (1978, p. 55) introduction to 'imaginative geography' supplies an explanation for the formation of stereotypes, describing how the mind 'dramatises' what is far away. This is especially true for nations associated with rural living and poverty, commonly due to westernised portrayals that lack appreciation for diversity. Examples of imaginative geography can be found in the two studies below.

- Before learning about India as part of a geography topic, students initially presented 'stereotypical, undifferentiated, and exotic answers' (Disney, 2005, p. 331) when asked to describe India; some children claimed that India did not have cars, buses, or modern technology. Interestingly, these attitudes changed after children were exposed to 'real experiences of real people' (Disney, 2005, p. 334) through a two-year project linked to a school in India.

- Students were asked to explain the attributes of their perceptions of Brazil; the most common answer was football and TV (Picton, 2008).

Although these were small-scale studies, the findings are important in emphasising the general idea of stereotyping when learning about distant places. They emphasise the 'well-placed' position of geography teachers in encouraging learning that accurately reflects distant cultures and challenges the persistent whiteness of geography education. In doing so, teachers' and students' critical cultural awareness is enhanced, reducing self and other perceptions when learning about distant places.

REFLECTION 8.2

How should the teachers in those two scenarios have reacted to ensure unhelpful and inaccurate perceptions of India and Brazil did not occur as the series of lessons progressed?

MEDIA INFLUENCE

The development of stereotypes, including negative images of the 'global south' and a derogatory viewpoint can stem from inadequate geography teaching. But media portrayals can also reinforce the *dependency culture* which presents western countries as superior in an economic relationship. For example, a Gambia relief poster could be used in discussions, like the images used by Comic Relief and Live Aid charity fundraisers, where the West's role in inequality is generally ignored. Media depictions are key players in the formation of stereotypes, often giving oversimplified accounts of complex problems such as poverty. It is unlikely that this is meant in a malicious way, it is simply an easier option. However, it results in a missed opportunity to portray distant places with cultural complexity.

DEVELOPING CRITICAL CULTURAL AWARENESS

Critical cultural awareness is an essential tool for managing stereotypes within the classroom. Their intercultural exploration, involving both secondary and primary research, understands the complicated and controversial nature of stereotyping, and thus the difficulties involved in challenging it. Developing this cultural competency enables children to critically evaluate perspectives and practices in their own and other cultures; in doing so it allows children to 'see who they are in relation to others'.

Critical cultural competence is a deep, nuanced and complex understanding of diversity that includes the skill of effectively communicating across cultures. This ability requires teachers to be reflective of their own knowledge to ensure that their practice meets the needs of every child, enhancing equity in education for all. Hence, the *Teachers' Standards* (DfE, 2011) require educators to demonstrate both good subject knowledge and the ability to respond to the needs of all pupils; these are both standards within the educational policy in England. And, as stereotyping is a common human practice, it is important for educators to develop these required competencies to effectively reduce the presence of 'exotic' perceptions in geography classrooms (Ofsted, 2011, p. 15).

A suggested method for becoming critically and culturally competent is to explicitly address existing stereotypes in the classroom. These discussions must be visual where possible, involving cultural dialogue and critical, transformative thinking opportunities that encourage geography learners to respect distant cultures/people. In doing so, geography teachers can demonstrate elements of *world-mindedness*, where global awareness encourages students to appreciate others' viewpoints and experiences; this conduct is necessary within Part 2 of the *Teachers' Standards* (DfE, 2011). World-mindedness in the classroom should include:

- enquiry into global issues;

- a conscious appreciation for culture;

- knowledge of interconnectedness;

- and improved 'habits of the mind' (open-mindedness, awareness of stereotypes and bias).

Utilising these suggestions, teachers can make the challenge of mastering critical cultural awareness into effective learning opportunities for primary geographers.

SUGGESTED AIMS FOR THE EFFECTIVE TEACHING OF DISTANT PLACES

The effective teaching of distant places in geography is extremely difficult. However, an inclusion of the global dimension can encourage children to make connections between local and global places. Although dated, incorporating the following eight key concepts is an effective way to do this: 'global citizenship, conflict resolution, diversity, human rights, interdependence, social justice, sustainable development, and values and perceptions' (DfES, 2005, p. 2). The global dimension encourages children to value diversity and understand 'the global context of their local lives' (DfES, 2005, p. 2), reflecting the national curriculum geography aims (DfE, 2013). The global dimension in geography learning also contributes to young people's geographical understanding, values and informed worldviews. When implementing the global dimension into classrooms, teachers should think about the connection between the role of global citizens and good educational practices. Practical teaching examples of this could include:

- structured enquiry;

- real experiences;

- scaffolded approaches to reflect on self and other;

- willingness to instantly address misconceptions as one would in a mathematics lesson;

- choice, where possible, to choose a distant place that appeals to the learner;

- role-play; and

- the use of photographs, artefacts, books and stories.

These practices are fundamental in supporting students' geographical thinking and the promotion of transformational geography, where education is part of a progressive, cultural change to reject stereotypes.

FOSTERING INCLUSIVE COMMUNITIES IN CLASSROOMS

So far, this chapter has looked at how learning about distant places in a critically culturally aware way can help children better understand distant places. It can also foster a better understanding of various ethnicities and cultures represented in their school or class. Creating a sense of belonging in globalised communities does not just have to occur in geography lessons and can be effectively achieved through the use of representative classroom resources that actively combat stereotypes across the curriculum and through the school ethos. By integrating diverse materials and resources into the classroom that reflect a wide range of cultures and languages, teachers can create an inclusive environment where all pupils see themselves represented and valued. Adapting the curriculum and using resources, such as multicultural books, films and artefacts that highlight the histories and cultures of various other cultures, can challenge preconceived ideas that pupils may hold about other countries and can also promote an awareness and understanding for other cultures and empathy for people from other cultures. Planning for collaborative activities and discussions centred around these resources and discussion points can encourage pupils to share their own stories and perspectives, fostering mutual respect and a deeper connection between pupils from diverse cultures. Additionally, inviting guest speakers and organising celebratory days for other cultures can further enrich pupil understanding, helping them appreciate the richness of diversity of the UK and reinforcing their sense of belonging in a globalised community.

Evidence from a local primary school found that the school has recently introduced a *cultural calendar*, aimed at celebrating and bookmarking special days for a variety of cultures. Alongside planning special days and activities to encourage pupils to learn about and understand these other cultures, children whose families celebrate such events would speak in assembly to explain their cultural traditions and how they celebrate.

This is all well and good to an extent; however, these specific days can be seen as tokenistic, where events like this are planned to 'keep up appearances' to show that the school is celebrating cultural diversity, rather than cultural diversity being integrated into the school's everyday life. Of course, this has to start somewhere and perhaps, with time, understanding and celebrating cultural diversity may assimilate with school life more seamlessly.

8 Globalisation and environmental deprivation

Now that we have considered effective teaching strategies linked with teaching about distant places, let's consider how we can teach the very children who may be present in our classrooms as a result of conflict in our globalised world.

REFUGEE AND ASYLUM SEEKER CHILDREN

Numerous scenarios, such as war, poverty and persecution, can precipitate people to seek refuge in another country. Globalisation has facilitated the movement of such migrants further afield and the UK is currently seen as a place of refuge by people from many countries for various reasons. Recent events, such as the war in Ukraine, has seen a rise in people seeking asylum in the UK, meaning schools are increasingly needing support in helping provide a quality education for children who arrive with limited resources financially, socially and emotionally. Teachers are competing with language barriers, but also potentially months or years of missed education. As of 2018, globally, there were 4 million refugee children out of school, missing out on their human right of education due to displacement, poverty or exclusion. Some of these children are particularly vulnerable; worryingly, in the year ending September 2022, the UK received 5,152 applications for asylum from unaccompanied children (Refugee Council, 2024).

Refugees who are displaced to a new host country most likely become an ethnic minority. Therefore, the reconstruction of their identity is key in integrating with mainstream society (Moghaddam, 2002). Refugee children face further challenges when placed into the UK school system. These four issues include:

- psychological well-being of refugee children;

- struggle to learn the new language of instruction;

- limited capacity to catch up without targeted support; and

- lack of professional development and support for teachers.

CHALLENGES FACED BY REFUGEE PUPILS

Before children and their families can obtain refugee status, they need to have their asylum claim processed. Although this timeframe should be about six months, it can sometimes take years, causing uncertainty for the child and stigma, due to perceived negative connotations of asylum seekers, by some factions.

Refugee children in the UK often face significant challenges with their education. Language barriers are a primary obstacle, as many arrive with limited or no proficiency in English,

128

making it difficult to access curriculum and communicate with fellow pupils and teachers. The trauma of displacement and the stress of adapting to an unfamiliar environment can also hinder their concentration and academic performance. Additionally, gaps in their prior education due to fleeing conflict zones can result in them being behind their peers academically. Social integration poses another hurdle, as these children may encounter bullying or feel isolated due to cultural differences. Additionally, navigating the UK's education system can be daunting for new pupils and their families, further complicating the family's ability to support their children's learning.

Numerous other financial hurdles exist for new arrivals, leading to children growing up in economic depression:

- asylum seekers are not allowed to work and are given £40 per week per person in the family, meaning many of these children are in extreme economic hardship;

- although housing is provided, asylum seekers do not have a choice in this; the quality can often be inadequate and it is often overcrowded;

- even when an asylum claim is processed, refugees may have limited work opportunities due to lack of English skills.

Of course, environmental deprivation such as pollution, lack of green spaces and unsafe living conditions can be faced by children of all ethnic backgrounds and nationalities (also explored in Chapter 2). For new arrivals, this deprivation further exacerbates these challenges by affecting children's health and ability to concentrate and perform well academically. Exposure to environmental hazards can lead to chronic health issues, increased absenteeism and cognitive impairments, all of which hinder educational attainment. Moreover, children in deprived environments often face psychological stress and instability, which can negatively affect their academic motivation and performance. Addressing these issues requires comprehensive policies that ensure equitable distribution of educational resources and the creation of healthy, safe learning environments for all children.

REFLECTION 8.3

Have you had experiences of working with refugee children?

Have you felt confident in supporting them?

Do you know how to access further support to help you and the children in your class?

8 Globalisation and environmental deprivation

CASE STUDY 8.2

Refugee Children

Harry, the head teacher of a large primary school in Staffordshire, was aware that the school was not prepared to best support refugee and asylum seeker children following a significant number of children fleeing from the Ukraine and Syria and becoming pupils at his school.

Although the school had been promoting a broadly inclusive ethos for as long as Harry had worked at the school, he felt a much more targeted approach was needed to support the new pupils. Although there was an existing and very competent EAL lead in the school, Harry recognised that language issues were not the only challenges these children faced. Speaking to head teachers in a cluster of schools he worked with, he heard about *schools of sanctuary*, schools that foster a culture of welcome and safety for people seeking sanctuary, including asylum seeking and refugee families. Harry learnt that to be recognised as a school of sanctuary, schools must demonstrate that the whole school community has learnt about migration issues, embedded policies and practices of welcome and inclusion, and shared their learning and efforts with the wider community and schools of sanctuary network. As a first step he downloaded the free resource pack from the Schools of Sanctuary website (details of which can be found in the Further reading section of this chapter). Harry understood that before officially becoming a school of sanctuary, a school has to provide evidence of meeting all the eight criteria set up by the organisation. He realised this would be a medium-term goal that the school could work towards, but wanted to be able to implement changes quickly. He decided to map out an action plan based on three themes of: learn, embed and share – which would involve teachers, pupils and families (see below) in pursuit of applying to be a school of sanctuary.

Table 8.1   Suggested action plan exemplifying school of sanctuary approach

Focus area	Staff	Pupils	Family
Learn	Staff were enrolled on two online learning courses over the course of the academic year (details of which can be found in the Further reading section of this chapter). *Who Counts as a Refugee?* Migrants and Refugees in Education	The whole school took part in Refugee Week, celebrating the achievements of various refugees, such as Mo Farah, and having a whole-school assembly each day that week focusing on refugees.	Signposting provided to the Parents' Immigration Action Group, which can educate parents about their rights and entitlements.

130

8 Globalisation and environmental deprivation

Focus area	Staff	Pupils	Family
	The EAL and safeguarding leads supported staff in taking part in an audit to ensure there were structures to identify and support students with EAL and those with emotional or trauma-related issues. Free resources from the Bell Foundation were shared with teachers and other school staff.	The English lead planned a unit of work based around the graphic novel *The Arrival* by Shaun Tan for Years 5 and 6.	
Embed	All staff, including lunchtime assistants, caretaker and parent-helpers, have a half-termly workshop with EAL lead to be shown how to use some of the interventions for refugee children. Any staff who would like to learn more can be provided with more training so that teachers are not the only staff who can support refugee children.	Subject leads to look for opportunities to engage further.	Parents and families from all backgrounds are invited to a culture café each week to make connections with other parents and collaborate on craft activities.
Share	A specific part of the staff meeting each fortnight is ring-fenced to discuss the school of sanctuary application and work to support becoming more inclusive, ensuring and sharing success stories from each class as well as challenges. Share activities and work via social media – for example, tweeting the Schools of Sanctuary account.	Children collaborate on piece of artwork at the school gates to show and reflect how the school is welcoming to all children including creating displays with the word 'welcome' in different languages.	Half-termly PTA meeting with interpreters to create shared plans for the school.

Once the action plan was up and running, Harry felt the school was a genuinely more welcoming environment and that staff who had been anxious, and sometimes even negative, about new arrivals in their class now felt empowered and eager to learn more to ensure a more equitable offer for children.

8 Globalisation and environmental deprivation

HOW CAN TEACHERS SUPPORT REFUGEE PUPILS FURTHER?

Save the Children (2018) has suggested recommendations for action to help refugee children transition more smoothly. Teachers can help them by creating a supportive and inclusive classroom environment tailored to their unique needs. Here are several strategies:

1. *Language support*: Provide EAL programmes and employ bilingual aides/teaching assistants to help refugee children overcome language barriers.

2. *Trauma-informed practices*: Understand the potential psychological impact of displacement and trauma, and create a safe, predictable classroom environment. Implement practices that address emotional and mental well-being, such as counselling services and peer support groups.

3. *Cultural sensitivity*: Educate themselves and their students about the cultural backgrounds of refugee children to foster an inclusive atmosphere. Celebrate cultural diversity through classroom activities and discussions to help refugee children feel valued and respected.

4. *Academic support*: Offer additional academic support through tutoring, homework clubs and personalised learning plans to help refugee children catch up on any educational gaps they may have.

5. *Parental engagement*: Engage with the families of refugee children by providing translated materials, interpreters for parent–teacher meetings and involving them in school activities. This helps create a supportive community network for the child.

6. *Collaboration with agencies*: Work closely with local refugee support organisations and community groups to provide comprehensive assistance and resources for refugee children and their families.

On a practical level, it is often the language barriers faced by refugee children which are an immediate barrier to learning and socialisation. For most refugee children, mastering the new language is the key to unlocking what they already know, and many teachers often struggle to support this process. With that in mind, teachers can use a range of resources and strategies, including:

- dual coding: combining visual (image-based) and verbal (language-based) elements to convey information;

- flash cards and visual timelines;

- key vocabulary for the lesson translated into their first language (Google translate app is good for this);

132

8 Globalisation and environmental deprivation

- considering how learning objectives can be shared, depending on level of English proficiency of the children;

- using drawings to help explain a word or concept;

- using videos and picture books (with limited text) instead of always using longer texts;

- implementing multilingual signage including Makaton;

- incorporating their native language into lessons (Google translate app is good for this as well);

- assisting understanding of second-language acquisition through professional development sessions for teachers.

Many of the above are features of a quality first teaching (QFT) approach anyway, which means they are beneficial not only for EAL children, but also for all children including those with SEN.

While there are clear differences between refugee EAL children and non-refugee (or asylum seeker) children in terms of their overall needs, the same language approaches can be used for both refugee and non-refugee EAL pupils. An initial first step is to really get to know the pupil and their family to understand the scale of their language and learning needs. The following resource can be useful here.

SAMPLE QUESTIONS TO GATHER MORE INFORMATION ABOUT REFUGEE CHILDREN AND THEIR FAMILIES (EAL)

Family background

- Was the child born in the UK?

- What is the country of origin/religion of the family?

- What is the child's native language?

Ask the following questions if the child does not speak English at home

- Is this the language the child uses at home?

- To whom and in what context?

- Does the child use English (target language) at home?

- To whom and in what context?

- Does the child watch English television/videos?

133

8 Globalisation and environmental deprivation

- Does the child watch videos in any other language?

- What does the father/mother do for a living?

- When did they move into the area? What is the reason for moving?

- Is the family home rented or privately owned?

- Who will help the child with homework?

- Is there a computer or laptop at home? Who is in charge of it? Does the mother know how to operate it?

- How many children are there in the family? Does the child have his/her own bedroom?

English and maths

- Make a note of the child's educational journey – dates and schools in and out of the UK; see if there are any gaps in the education; don't forget to comment on that – topics that may need to be covered through extra interventions.

- Depending on the year group – ask the child about the common English and Maths topics; note down what they find difficult and would need help with.

- Check if they know their timetables, counting, four operations in mathematics, alphabets and sounds, books they read at home (if any), ask them about their favourite characters – make a note if they could talk about it at length.

- What is the child's routine at home in terms of education?

- Check the school languages database (if applicable) to see which staff member would be able to help if the child does not speak English at the time of admission; mention it in the notes.

- If unsure of the literacy skills, select a book for the child to read; comment on it in the final notes.

- Ask the child if they know about their previous levels in school.

- Comment about the assessment to be used for the child.

School information

- Discuss the home school diary, reading record, school gates, etc.

- Behaviour policy for the school.

- Medical needs if any; involve school nurses if needed.

- If the child is coming from another country explain what to do if they feel that they are being bullied, racially abused or harassed by other children in the playground – for example, they don't understand the accent. They must tell the class teacher or the adult who speaks their language straight away and never take matters in their own hands (never hit or abuse verbally).

- School uniform; what and where to buy dinner; school dinners or packed lunch; no sugary foods allowed; give examples of healthy foods that parents can buy from supermarkets.

Parents' literacy skills

- Do the parents speak or understand English?

- If not, please ask if they have a friend who can translate for them; note down their phone number.

- Are they interested in parent learning classes; if yes, take contact details.

- Is there a need for letters from school to be translated?

- Can the parents read with their children?

- Comment on how enthusiastic the parents are to help with their children's education.

- How settled are the parents in the community?

- Would they need help with anything else outside the school? Tell them what the school can do to help.

(Adapted from Maude, 2023)

Schools may also be able to help with some of the issues facing refugees due to environmental deprivation. Certainly, all schools, regardless of the physical support they can provide, should have a non-judgemental attitude and an understanding attitude to classroom behaviour caused by lack of sleep and/or hunger, such as inattentiveness. Further suggestions include:

- free daily breakfast clubs;

- help providing uniform, shoes and basic equipment through donations;

- applying for grants to be able to provide families with bedding;

- holding employability and language workshops at the school premises for parents/carers.

Teachers can prepare all children for an increasingly globalised world by equipping them with the skills and knowledge necessary to thrive in diverse, interconnected environments. This approach directly supports refugee, asylum seeker and EAL children, but also indirectly supports them by ensuring their classmates are welcoming. Teachers can do this through fostering critical thinking, problem-solving abilities and adaptability through interactive and collaborative learning experiences. Emphasising the importance of cultural competence and empathy, teachers can introduce students to various cultures, languages and global issues, encouraging an appreciation for diversity and creating a sense of global citizenship. Incorporating technology into the classroom can also enhance pupils' digital literacy, broadening their skills. Additionally, promoting multilingualism and offering opportunities for international exchange programmes in secondary school can further prepare pupils for global engagement. By creating an inclusive, forward-thinking school environment, teachers can help pupils develop the skills and mindset needed to navigate and contribute positively to a globalised society. Table 8.2 can help teachers self-audit their class for inclusivity.

Table 8.2   Inclusive classroom strategy checklist (adapted from Maude, 2023)

Strategies supportive and inclusive of EAL learner	In place in class	Included in own planning	Not applicable to class
Creating a supportive environment			
• get to know pupil as an individual: their background, experiences, interests, skills, approaches to learning			
• ensure correct pronunciation and spelling of pupils' names			
• encourage and seek opportunities to use first language at appropriate stages of learning			
• create an environment free of harassment, where each student feels valued and safe			
• actively model and encourage an atmosphere of risk-taking in an environment where errors are seen as a natural and important part of learning			
Providing an inclusive curriculum			
• select content, texts, examples and illustrations which include and reflect the diversity of pupil backgrounds			

Strategies supportive and inclusive of EAL learner	In place in class	Included in own planning	Not applicable to class
• consciously interact with pupils, supporting them to make connections to and build on previous learning and experiences			
• strategically use a variety of grouping techniques and peer tutoring			
• provide extended waiting time to allow pupils time to process the question and their response			
• monitor pupil understanding, providing opportunity for individual explanations and support where needed			
• build up shared 'class' experiences to draw upon			
Teaching to support English-language development			
• explicitly teach the technical subject-specific language			
• clarify key words, rephrase key content in a variety of ways, provide both written and oral forms of key words			
• use non-verbal cues and concrete and visual materials alongside language			
• use group work effectively where pupils use language to complete purposeful, cognitively demanding tasks			

CONCLUSION

In recent decades, globalisation has been a catalyst for change in almost all domains of life, from economics and politics to technology and communication. It has also brought about increasing mobility of people, including children across the world. Increasing opportunities to travel, as well interconnectedness due to the internet, means pupils need to be taught about distant places in a critical and culturally aware way which mitigates against negative stereotype formation.

8 Globalisation and environmental deprivation

Meanwhile, migration to the UK, particularly with regards to refugee and asylum seeker children, means schools need to be more inclusive. Teachers need to embrace developing a cross-cultural skill set. Head teachers, like the one described in the case study, need to update school policies and develop action plans in order to respond to these global impact changes. By implementing the strategies detailed in this chapter, teachers can help refugee children integrate more smoothly into their new educational environment and support their overall development and well-being, at the same time giving all children a deeper understanding of the wider world.

CHAPTER SUMMARY

This chapter has so far considered:

- how a sense of belonging can be fostered in globalised communities by drawing upon representative classroom resources which combat stereotypes;

- living with diversity demands skills and competencies to balance the need to share common spaces and experiences with the need to maintain separate identities;

- managing the impact of globalisation through local innovation – for example, setting up a children's forum to create public art projects, encouraging ethnic minority participation in football, etc.

FURTHER READING AND RESOURCES

Critical Cultural Awareness: Managing Stereotypes Through Intercultural (Language) Education by
S. A. Houghton, F. Yumiko, M. Lebedko and S. Li (2013)

This book is a valuable resource in developing understanding of the nature of stereotypes; it suggests ways in which teachers can manage them by developing critical cultural awareness as an intrinsic part of the intercultural communicative competence of their students.

Who Counts as a Refugee?

OpenLearn – Open University

www.open.edu/openlearn/society-politics-law/geography/who-counts-refugee/content-section-0?active-tab=description-tab

Migrants and Refugees in Education

Online Course – FutureLearn

www.futurelearn.com/courses/working-supportively-with-refugees

Welcoming Refugee and Asylum-Seeking Learners

Bell Foundation

www.bell-foundation.org.uk/resources/guidance/schools-and-leaders/welcoming-refugee-and-asylum-seeking-learners/

This website provides a selection of the most relevant documents to support schools in understanding and meeting the needs of refugee and asylum-seeking children.

Schools of Sanctuary resource pack https://cdn.cityofsanctuary.org/uploads/sites/159/2021/11/Schools-of-Sanctuary-Resource-Pack.pdf

This pack shares and celebrates just a glimpse of the amazing work going on in schools around the country today and provides plenty of practical tips to begin your journey to being recognised as a school of sanctuary.

UNHCR publications

https://reporting.unhcr.org/publications#tab-global_report

On this page you will find UNHCR's reports, appeals, funding updates, factsheets and other types of publications from its operations worldwide.

Teaching resources

British Red Cross

www.redcross.org.uk/get-involved/teaching-resources

This page presents free teaching resources to help enrich curriculum subjects and connect human crisis with human kindness.

Refugee Council

www.refugeecouncil.org.uk/

This website provides information about how the work undertaken by the Refugee Council transforms the lives of refugees and people seeking asylum.

CONCLUDING REMARKS

KULWINDER MAUDE

Writing a book on the role of diversity, equity and inclusion (DEI) in teaching for primary school teachers has been an important endeavour for several compelling reasons – from enhancing teacher understanding and competence to supporting a long-term systemic change in society. We hope that this book will serve as a comprehensive guide and resource, helping teaching and non-teaching staff in school to understand and implement DEI principles effectively in their classrooms. We sincerely hope that by reading this book and following the suggestions given you will feel empowered as a teacher in shaping young lives for the world of tomorrow in the following ways.

ENHANCING TEACHER UNDERSTANDING AND COMPETENCE

- *Educational foundation*: This book, dedicated to DEI, provides teachers with a thorough understanding of the concepts and principles of diversity, equity and inclusion. We have explained the theoretical underpinnings (where applicable) and presented practical suggestions through case studies and reflective questions, to help teachers grasp the importance of these principles in the educational context.

- *Professional development*: Continuous professional development is crucial for teachers. This book serves as a professional development tool, offering DEI-targeted strategies, insights and case studies that teachers can use to enhance their skills and effectiveness in managing diverse classrooms.

ADDRESSING CLASSROOM DIVERSITY

- *Diverse student populations*: Classrooms today are increasingly diverse, with children from various cultural, linguistic, socio-economic and ability backgrounds. This provides teachers with strategies to understand and meet the needs of all their pupils, ensuring that every child feels valued and included.

- *Cultural competence*: Teachers need to develop cultural competence to effectively teach students from different backgrounds. We offer practical advice on how to foster cultural awareness and sensitivity, helping teachers create an inclusive learning environment.

PROMOTING EQUITY IN EDUCATION

- *Reducing achievement gaps*: Equity-focused teaching practices are essential for addressing and reducing achievement gaps among pupils. We highlight the importance of equitable and inclusive teaching methods and provide actionable strategies for teachers to implement in their classrooms.

- *Individualised teaching*: Recognising that each child has unique needs, through this book we guide our teachers on how to tailor their teaching and learning strategies to support every child's learning journey. This individualised approach can help remove barriers to learning and promote academic success for all pupils.

FOSTERING INCLUSIVE CLASSROOMS

- *Creating a sense of belonging*: An inclusive classroom environment is one where all children feel they belong and are respected. This book offers insights on how to cultivate such an environment, emphasising the importance of respect, empathy and positive relationships among all children.

- *Encouraging pupil voice*: Inclusion involves giving all pupils a voice in their educational journey. We provide strategies for teachers to encourage pupil participation and ensure that all voices are heard and valued in the classroom.

PREPARING CHILDREN FOR A DIVERSE WORLD

- *Global competence*: As children are growing up in an increasingly interconnected world, they need to develop skills to navigate and appreciate diversity. The DEI focus of this book helps teachers prepare pupils for this reality by incorporating global perspectives and promoting intercultural understanding.

- *Building social-emotional skills*: Understanding and appreciating diversity helps children build critical social-emotional skills such as empathy, collaboration and respect for others. This book provides guidance on how to integrate these skills into the curriculum.

SUPPORTING SYSTEMIC CHANGE

- *Advocating for social justice*: Teachers play a key role in promoting social justice through education. We hope this book will empower teachers to become advocates for systemic change, equipping them with the knowledge and tools to challenge inequities and promote social justice within and beyond the classroom.

9 Concluding remarks

- *Inspiring continuous improvement*: Through this dedicated resource on DEI, we hope teachers will be inspired to continuously reflect on and improve their teaching practices, encouraging a mindset of lifelong learning and adaptation – essential for effectively addressing the evolving needs of diverse pupil populations.

HIGHLIGHTS

This section presents highlights from individual chapters and reminds readers about what they have learnt from each chapter.

Chapter 1 addressed racism in primary schools, advocating a proactive, informed and compassionate approach. Teachers play a pivotal role in shaping students' attitudes and behaviours towards race and diversity. By educating themselves and their students, creating inclusive environments, promoting empathy and respect, addressing incidents of racism promptly, building supportive communities, implementing clear policies and engaging in reflective practice, teachers can effectively tackle racism and contribute to a more equitable and inclusive society. Several strategies were suggested to tackle racism, such as: educating and developing awareness about the role of an inclusive environment; engaging with social-emotional learning through PSHE; developing clear policies and procedures to report and monitor racist incidences; developing restorative practices to help children understand the impact of their actions; and encouraging teachers to engage with reflective practice as a part of CPD.

Chapter 2 addressed economic injustice in society, promoting a multifaceted approach that includes creating an inclusive classroom environment, supporting children's basic needs, engaging parents and communities, understanding the impact of policy change, providing equitable educational opportunities, and encouraging social justice and advocacy – all in the primary classroom. By understanding the complexities of economic injustice and implementing the strategies suggested in the chapter, teachers can help mitigate its impact on students and contribute to a more equitable and just society. Teachers have learnt more about the role of Pupil Premium and FSMs in closing the attainment gap for children from economically disadvantaged backgrounds.

Chapter 3 addressed gender discrimination and sexism in schools through a comprehensive approach that involves promoting gender equity in the classroom, encouraging equal participation, providing diverse role models, addressing biases and stereotypes, creating a supportive environment, engaging parents and communities, advocating for policy change and promoting critical thinking and awareness. By understanding the complexities of gender discrimination and implementing these strategies, teachers can create a more inclusive and equitable learning environment for all children. Teachers are encouraged to promote gender equity in the classroom by ensuring that the curriculum reflects diverse contributions from all genders and challenges traditional gender roles. Further changes can be made by being mindful of classroom dynamics and ensuring that all pupils have equal opportunities to participate in discussions and activities – avoiding calling on children based on gender and addressing any patterns of unequal participation. Mixed-gender group work can be encouraged to promote collaboration and reduce gender-based segregation in classroom activities.

Chapter 4 addressed exclusion through disability in schools, advocating for a multifaceted approach that includes creating an inclusive classroom environment, differentiating teaching and learning, fostering social inclusion, participating in professional development, building a supportive school culture, engaging families and communities, and continuously monitoring and evaluating practices. By understanding the unique challenges faced by children with disabilities and implementing these strategies, teachers can help create a more equitable and inclusive educational experience for all students. We discussed how CPD training programmes can help build understanding of the diverse needs of pupils with disabilities and considered effective strategies for inclusion.

Chapter 5 enlightened teachers about the concepts of ableism and neuronormativity in schools. Through case studies and explicit strategies, inclusive education practices were introduced, as well as those fostering a supportive classroom environment, providing necessary accommodations, promoting awareness and education, creating a collaborative community, addressing bias and stereotypes, and monitoring and evaluating efforts. By understanding and implementing these strategies, teachers can create a more equitable and inclusive educational experience for all children, ensuring that every child has the opportunity to thrive.

Chapter 6 focused on supporting the development of communal identity in schools through an inclusive and respectful environment that acknowledges and celebrates cultural diversity. By implementing culturally responsive teaching practices, engaging families and communities, supporting multilingualism, promoting social cohesion, addressing biases, providing supportive resources and promoting student voice, teachers can help children feel valued and connected to their cultural heritage. This, in turn, enhances their sense of belonging, self-esteem and overall well-being, contributing to a positive and inclusive school culture.

Chapter 7 proposed that supporting personal identity in schools involves creating an inclusive environment, adopting culturally responsive teaching practices, encouraging self-expression, promoting social-emotional learning, building strong relationships, providing supportive resources, engaging families and communities, addressing biases and promoting student voice and leadership. By understanding and implementing these strategies, teachers can help children develop a strong sense of self, leading to greater self-esteem, better mental health and social cohesion.

Chapter 8 addressed global challenges, starting with the need to teach about distant places in a critically culturally aware approach to negate stereotype formation. Specific ways were suggested for integrating relevant issues into the curriculum, supporting affected refugee children, encouraging community action if possible, engaging families and communities, addressing socio-economic disparities and monitoring impact on children in our classrooms. By implementing these strategies, teachers can help their pupils understand and address critical global and environmental issues, fostering a sense of responsibility and preparing them to contribute positively to their communities and the world.

CONCLUSION

In summary, writing a book on the role of diversity, equity and inclusion in teaching for primary school teachers is a crucial step towards enhancing educational practices and outcomes. It is hoped this book provides valuable knowledge, practical strategies and inspiration for teachers, helping them create equitable and inclusive learning environments that support the success and well-being of all children.

REFERENCES

CHAPTER 1

DfE (2010) *Equality Act*. Available at: https://assets.publishing.service.gov.uk/media/5a7e3237 ed915d74e33f0ac9/Equality_Act_Advice_Final.pdf. Accessed 28 August 2024.

DfE (2012) *School Strategies for Preventing and Tackling Bullying*. Available at: www.gov.uk/government/publications/school-strategies-for-preventing-and-tackling-bullying. Accessed 29 August 2024.

DfE (2013) *Ethnic Minority Achievement*. London: DfE.

Geoghegan, S. (2022) *End Violence Against Women*. Available at: www.endviolenceagainstwomen.org.uk/almost-half-of-women-have-less-trust-in-police-following-sarah-everard-murder/. Accessed 27 August 2024.

Gillborn, D. (2005) Education policy as an act of white supremacy: whiteness, critical race theory and education reform. *Journal of Education Policy*, *20*(4): 485–505.

Gillborn, D. (2024) *White Lies: Racism, Education and Critical Race Theory*. Oxford: Taylor & Francis.

gov.uk (2022) *Inclusive Britain: Government Response to the Commission on Race and Ethnic Disparities*. Available at: www.gov.uk/government/publications/inclusive-britain-action-plan-government-response-to-the-commission-on-race-and-ethnic-disparities. Accessed 29 August 2024.

Khan, O. (2020) The colour of money. *The Cognitive Behaviour Therapist*, *3*. Available at: www.runnymedetrust.org/blog/the-colour-ofmoney-race-and-economic-inequality. Accessed 10 September 2024.

Lander, V. and Smith, H. (2024) *An Anti-Racist Framework for Initial Teacher Education and Training*. Centre for Race, Education and Decoloniality, Leeds. Available at: www.leedsbeckett.ac.uk/blogs/carnegie-education/2022/11/anti-racism-framework/. Accessed 10 September 2024.

Phillips, T. (2005) *After 7/7: Sleepwalking to Segregation*. Speech given as Chair of the Commission for Racial Equality. Manchester.

Race Disparity Unit (RDU) (2022, 7 April) *Why We No Longer Use the Term 'BAME' in Government*. Available at: https://equalities.blog.gov.uk/2022/04/07/why-we-no-longer-use-the-term-bame-in-government/. Accessed 27 August 2024.

Sapouna, M., de Amicis, L. and Vezzali, L. (2023) Bullying victimization due to racial, ethnic, citizenship and/or religious status: a systematic review. *Adolescent Research Review*, 8: 261–96. https://doi.org/10.1007/s40894-022-00197-2

Schuelka, M. J. (2018) Implementing inclusive education. *K4D Helpdesk Report*. Brighton: Institute of Development Studies.

References

Shah, N. and Coles, J. A. (2020) Preparing teachers to notice race in classrooms: contextualizing the competencies of preservice teachers with antiracist inclinations. *Journal of Teacher Education, 71*(5): 584–99.

Shutti, G., Healey, A., Pierce, J. and Baxter, R. (2020) How stop and search in the UK is failing black people. *Guardian*. Available at: www.theguardian.com/law/video/2020/jul/07/does-stop-and-search-in-the-uk-need-to-change-video-explainer. Accessed 27 August 2024.

CHAPTER 2

Action for Children (2024) *Where is Child Poverty Increasing in the UK?* Available at: www.action-forchildren.org.uk/blog/where-is-child-poverty-increasing-in-the-uk/?utm_source=dm.google&utm_medium=cpc&utm_term=grant%20account%20blog&utm_content=child%20poverty%20increasing%20in%20the%20UK&gad_source=1&gclid=Cj0KCQjw0Oq2BhCCARIsAA5hubXClmhvr5N8W41JRG-nQIGD7eMatMc_1CcTvKDy_67LoV_Y8H2dWoQaApOfEALw_wcB. Accessed 11 September 2024.

American Psychological Association (APA) (2024) *Socioeconomic Status*. Available at: www.apa.org/topics/socioeconomic-status. Accessed 13 September 2024.

Clarke, C., Bonnet, B., Flores, M. and Thévenon, O. (2022) The economic costs of childhood socio-economic disadvantage in European OECD countries. *OECD Papers on Well-being and Inequalities*, No. 9. Paris: OECD. https://doi.org/10.1787/8c0c66b9-en

Coleman, J. S. (1966) Equality of Educational Opportunity (COLEMAN) Study (EEOS). *Inter-university Consortium for Political and Social Research [distributor], 2007-04-27*. https://doi.org/10.3886/ICPSR06389.v3

Copeland, J. (2018) A critical reflection on the reasoning behind, and effectiveness of, the application of the Pupil Premium grant within primary schools. *Management in Education, 33*(2): 70–6.

DfE (2019) *ITT Core Content Framework*. Available at: assets.publishing.service.gov.uk/media/6061eb9cd3bf7f5cde260984/ITT_core_content_framework_.pdf. Accessed 2 September 2024.

Diemer, M. A., Mistry, R. S., Wadsworth, M. E., López, I. and Reimers, F. (2013) Best practices in conceptualizing and measuring social class in psychological research. *Analyses of Social Issues and Public Policy, 13*(1): 77–113.

Dräger, J., Klein, M. and Sosu, E. (2023) The long-term consequences of early school absences for educational attainment and labour market outcomes. *British Educational Research Journal, 50*: 1636–54. https://doi.org/10.1002/berj.3992

Education Endowment Foundation (EEF) (2021) *Impact of COVID-19 School Closures and Subsequent Support Strategies on Attainment and Socioemotional Wellbeing in Key Stage 1.* Available at: https://educationendowmentfoundation.org.uk/projects-and-evaluation/projects/nfer-impact-of-school-closures-and-subsequent-support-strategies-on-attainment-and-socioemotional-wellbeing-in-key-stage-1. Accessed 27 August 2024.

Gorard, S. and Siddiqui, N. (2019) How trajectories of disadvantage help explain school attainment. *Sage Open, 9*(1): 2158244018825171.

Gorard, S., Siddiqui, N. and See, B. H. (2021) The difficulties of judging what difference the Pupil Premium has made to school intakes and outcomes in England. *Research Papers in Education, 36*(3), 355–79. https://doi.org/10.1080/02671522.2019.1677759

gov.uk (2023a) *Early Years Foundation Stage Profile Results, Academic Year 2022/23.* Available at: https://explore-education-statistics.service.gov.uk/find-statistics/early-years-foundation-stage-profile-results. Accessed 22 July 2024.

gov.uk (2023b) *Early Years Foundation Stage Statutory Framework.* Available at: https://assets.publishing.service.gov.uk/media/65aa5e42ed27ca001327b2c7/EYFS_statutory_framework_for_group_and_school_based_providers.pdf. Accessed 1 September 2024.

gov.uk (2023c) *Multiplication Tables Check Attainment, Academic Year 2022/23.* Available at: https://explore-education-statistics.service.gov.uk/find-statistics/multiplication-tables-check-attainment. Accessed 16 August 2024.

Hutchings, M. (2021) Inequality, social mobility and the 'glass floor': how more affluent parents secure educational advantage for their children. *Educational Research for Social Justice: Evidence and Practice from the UK* (pp. 137–69). Cham: Springer International.

Ingleby, E. (2021) *Neoliberalism Across Education.* New York: Springer International.

Joseph Rountree Foundation (2024) *UK Poverty 2024.* Available at: www.jrf.org.uk/uk-poverty-2024-the-essential-guide-to-understanding-poverty-in-the-uk. Accessed 28 August 2024.

Maslow, A. H. (1943) Hierarchy of Needs. *Psychological Review, 50*: 370–96.

Mazzoli Smith, L. and Todd, L. (2019) Conceptualising poverty as a barrier to learning through 'poverty proofing the school day': the genesis and impacts of stigmatisation. *British Educational Research Journal, 45*(2): 356–71.

National Housing Federation (2021) *1 in 5 Children in Need of a New Home.* Available at: www.housing.org.uk/news-and-blogs/news/1-in-5-children-need-new-home/. Accessed 2 September 2024.

OECD (2011) *Against the Odds: Disadvantaged Students Who Succeed in School.* PISA, Paris. Available at: https://doi.org/10.1787/9789264090873-en. Accessed 11 September 2024.

Ofsted (2019) *School Inspection Update.* Available at: https://assets.publishing.service.gov.uk/media/5c41e555ed915d38a6a87aeb/School_inspection_update_-_January_2019_Special_Edition_180119.pdf. Accessed 27 August 2024.

Reiss, F. (2013) Socioeconomic inequalities and mental health problems in children and adolescents: a systematic review. *Social Science and Medicine, 90*: 24–31.

Safran, M. A., Mays Jr, R. A., Huang, L. N., McCuan, R., Pham, P. K., Fisher, S. K., McDuffie, K. Y. and Trachtenberg, A. (2009) Mental health disparities. *American Journal of Public Health, 99*(11): 1962–6.

Schools Week (2024) *Teaching assistants cut in 75% of primary schools.* Available at: https://schoolsweek.co.uk/teaching-assistants-cut-in-75-of-primary-schools/#:~:text=Three%2Dquarters%20of%20primary%20schools,activities%20are%20also%20being%20chopped. Accessed 28 August 2024.

Services for Education (2024) *Addressing the Silent Crisis: Children Missing in Education.* Available at: www.servicesforeducation.co.uk/blog/safeguarding/addressing-the-silent-crisis-children-missing-in-education/. Accessed 28 August 2024.

Social Mobility Commission (2020) *Annual Review and Business Plan 2020*. Available at: www.gov.uk/government/publications/social-mobility-commission-unveils-annual-review-2020. Accessed 11 September 2024.

Sutton Trust (2021) *A Fair Start? Equalising Access to Early Education*. Available at: www.suttontrust.com/wp-content/uploads/2021/08/Sutton-Trust-A-Fair-Start.pdf. Accessed 13 September 2024.

Understanding Society (2020) *Independent School Pupils Did Not Lose as Much Learning as State School Children During Lockdown*. Available here: www.understandingsociety.ac.uk/news/2020/10/28/independent-school-pupils-did-not-lose-as-much-learning-as-state-school-children-during-lockdown/. Accessed 28 August 2024.

CHAPTER 3

Bowler, M. (2020) Girls just want to learn languages? *HEPI*. Available at: www.hepi.ac.uk/2020/02/18/girls-just-want-to-learn-languages/. Accessed 11 September 2024.

Cawdell, S. (1999) *Strategies for Improving Boys' Academic Performance*. London: Teacher Training Agency.

Clark, C. and Douglas, J. (2011) *Young People's Reading and Writing*. London: National Literacy Trust.

Clark, C. and Rumbold, K. (2006) *Reading for Pleasure: A Research Overview*. London: National Literacy Trust.

Clark, C., Picton, I. and Galway, M. (2023) *Children and Young People's Reading in 2023*. London: National Literacy Trust.

Clark, C., Woodley, J. and Lewis, F. (2011) *The Gift of Reading in 2011: Children and Young People's Access to Books and Attitudes towards Reading*. London: National Literacy Trust.

Connolly, S. and Gregory, M. (2007) Women and work since 1970. In Crafts, N., Gazeley, I. and Newell, A. (eds), *Work and Pay in 20th Century Britain*. Oxford: Oxford University Press, p. 151.

Currie, D. H., Kelly, D. M. and Pomerantz, S. (2006) 'The geeks shall inherit the earth': girls' agency, subjectivity and empowerment. *Journal of Youth Studies*, 9(4): 419–36.

Davis, J. T. and Hines, M. (2020) How large are gender differences in toy preferences? A systematic review and meta-analysis of toy preference research. *Archives of Sexual Behavior*, 49(2): 373–94.

Department for Business, Innovation and Skills (BIS) (2016) *Fulfilling Our Potential: Teaching Excellence, Social Mobility and Student Choice*. Available at: assets.publishing.service.gov.uk/media/5a80cb7b40f0b62305b8d304/bis-16-261-he-green-paper-fulfilling-our-potential-summary-of-responses.pdf. Accessed 2 September 2024.

DfE (2012) *Research Evidence on Reading for Pleasure*. Available at: assets.publishing.service.gov.uk/media/5a7c18d540f0b61a825d66e9/reading_for_pleasure.pdf. Accessed 2 September 2024.

Epstein, D. (1998) *Failing Boys? Issues in Gender and Achievement*. London: McGraw-Hill Education.

Gender Trust (2024) *Gender Inequality in the British Education System*. Available at: www.gender-trust.org.uk/gender-inequality-in-the-british-education-system/. Accessed 11 September 2024.

Ghorfati, A. and Medini, R. (2015) *Feminism and its impact on woman in the modern society*. Unpublished MA dissertation. University of Tlemcen.

gov.uk (2023) *Key Stage 2 Attainment*. Available at: https://explore-education-statistics.service.gov.uk/find-statistics/key-stage-2-attainment. Accessed 2 September 2024.

Goodier, M. (2023) Gender gap shrinks and regional gap widens: 2023's key GCSE trends in England. *Guardian*. Available at: www.theguardian.com/education/2023/aug/24/gender-gap-shrinks-and-regional-gap-widens-2023-key-gcse-trends-in-england. Accessed 11 September 2024.

Gurian, M. and Stevens, K. (2005) *The Minds of Boys*. San Francisco, CA: Jossey-Bass.

Gurian, M., Stevens, K. and Daniels, P. (2009) Single-sex classrooms are succeeding. *Educational Horizons*, *87*(4): 234–45.

Houtte, M. V. (2004) Why boys achieve less at school than girls: the difference between boys' and girls' academic culture. *Educational Studies, 30*(2): 159–73.

Jackson, C. (2003) Motives for 'laddishness' at school: fear of failure and fear of the 'feminine'. *British Educational Research Journal, 29*(4): 583–98.

Kaman, M. R. (2015) Feminism and its impact on women in the modern society. *International Journal of Interdisciplinary Research in Science Society and Culture, 5*(2): 73–86.

LEGO Play Unstoppable (2024) *About us*. Available at: www.lego.com/en-gb/aboutus/news/2024/february/lego-play-unstoppable?locale=en-gb. Accessed 28 August 2024.

Martinez, T. (2022) *Gender neutral parenting: raising a generation outside the gender binary*. Doctoral dissertation. University of Arkansas.

McRobbie, A. (1997) More! New sexualities in girls' and women's magazines. In McRobbie (ed.), *Back to Reality? Social Experience and Cultural Studies* (pp. 190–209). Manchester: Manchester University Press.

Mead, M. (1935) *Sex and Temperament* (p. 280). London: Routledge and Kegan Paul.

Mitsos, E. and Browne, K. (1998) Gender differences in education: the underachievement of boys. *Sociology Review, 8*: 27–9.

Narsaria, A. (2019) Boy dolls: why dolls are considered misfit for boys? *Science ABC, 17 October*. Available at: www.scienceabc.com/social-science/why-are-boys-not-allowed-to-play-with-dolls.html. Accessed 28 August 2024.

Not Only Pink and Blue (n.d.) *Growing generations of equals*. Available at: www.notonlypinkandblue.com/. Accessed 10 July 2024.

Oakley, A. (ed.) (2005) *The Ann Oakley Reader: Gender, Women and Social Science*. London: Policy Press.

Ofsted (2011) *Girls' Career Aspirations*. Available at: https://assets.publishing.service.gov.uk/media/5a8183c9ed915d74e33fe9f2/Girls__career_aspirations.doc. Accessed 28 August 2024.

Pope, C. (2015) *The social and economic consequences of gendered toys in America*. University of Puget Sound.

Sharpe, S. (1976/1994) *Just Like A Girl*. London: Penguin.

Skelton, C., Francis, B. and Valkanova, Y. (2007) *Breaking Down the Stereotypes: Gender and Achievement in Schools*. Manchester: Equal Opportunities Commission.

UCAS (2016) *UCAS Data Reveals the Numbers of Men and Women Placed in Over 150 Higher Education Subjects*. Available at: www.ucas.com/corporate/news-and-key-documents/news/ucas-data-reveals-numbers-men-and-women-placed-over-150-higher. Accessed 2 September 2024.

Uncu, G. and Çalışır, G. (2018) Gender of colour: when did girls and boys start to wear pink and blue? *Studies on Balkan and Near Eastern Social Sciences*, 2: 281–7.

University of Plymouth (n.d.) *Why We Need More Men to Become Nurses*. Available at: www.plymouth.ac.uk/schools/school-of-nursing-and-midwifery/men-in-nursing. Accessed 2 September 2024.

US Bureau of Labor (2022) *Statistics*. Available at: www.bls.gov/. Accessed 2 September 2024.

YouGov (2017) *Boys' Toys are Seen as More Universal Than Girls' Toys*. Available at: https://today.yougov.com/politics/articles/19919-boys-toys-are-seen-more-universal-girls-toys. Accessed 10 July 2024.

CHAPTER 4

Ayala, E. C. (1999) 'Poor little things' and 'Brave little souls': The portrayal of individuals with disabilities in children's literature. *Literacy Research and Instruction*, 39(1): 103–17.

Beckett, A., Ellison, N., Barrett, S. and Shah, S. (2010) 'Away with the fairies?' Disability within primary-age children's literature. *Disability and Society*, 25(3): 373–86.

Booth, T. and Ainscow, M. (eds) (1998) *From Them to Us: An International Study of Inclusion in Education*. London: Routledge.

Cheyne, R. (2019) *Disability, Literature, Genre: Representation and Affect in Contemporary Fiction*. Liverpool: Liverpool University Press.

Cook, A. and Ogden, J. (2022) Challenges, strategies and self-efficacy of teachers supporting autistic pupils in contrasting school settings: a qualitative study. *European Journal of Special Needs Education*, 37(3): 371–85.

Darrow, A. (2006) *Sounds in the Silence: Research on Music and Deafness. Update. University of South Carolina. Department of Music*, 25(1): 5–14. https://doi.org/10.1177/87551233060250010102

Davis, J. M. and Watson, N. (2001) Where are the children's experiences? Analysing social and cultural exclusion in 'special' and 'mainstream' schools. *Disability and Society*, 16(5): 671–87.

Department of Health and Human Services (2015) Physical disabilities. *Better Health Channel*. Available at: www.betterhealth.vic.gov.au/health/servicesandsupport/physical-disabilities. Accessed 16 August 2024.

DfE (2010) *Equality Act*. Available at: https://assets.publishing.service.gov.uk/media/5a7e3237ed915d74e33f0ac9/Equality_Act_Advice_Final.pdf. Accessed 28 August 2024.

gov.uk (n.d.) *Equality Act 2010: Guidance*. Available at: www.gov.uk/guidance/equality-act-2010-guidance. Accessed 16 August 2024.

Independent Provider of Special Education Advice (IPSEA) (2024) Available at: www.ipsea.org.uk/. Accessed 11 September 2024.

Kearney, A. (2008) Exclusion at school: what is happening for students who are disabled? *International Journal of Diversity in Organizations, Communities, and Nations, 7*(6): 219.

Keil, S., Miller, O. and Cobb, R. (2006) Special educational needs and disability. *British Journal of Special Education, 33*(4): 168–72.

Long, R., Lewis, J., Danechi, S. and Powell, A. (2023) *The Special Educational Needs and Disabilities and Alternative Provision Improvement Plan*. House of Commons Library. Available at: https://researchbriefings.files.parliament.uk/documents/CBP-9760/CBP-9760.pdf. Accessed 11 September 2024.

National Deaf Children's Society (NDCS) (n.d.a) *Music Teaching for Deaf Children*. Available at: www.ndcs.org.uk/information-and-support/professionals/activities/music/. Accessed 28 August 2024.

NDCS (n.d.b) *What is Deafness? Main Types of Deafness*. Available at: www.ndcs.org.uk/information-and-support/childhood-deafness/what-is-deafness/. Accessed 28 August 2024.

Ridgway, R. (2016) Supporting deaf learners. In Waugh, D. and Walker-Gleaves, C. (eds), *Looking After Literacy*. London: Sage.

Robinson, D. (2017) Effective inclusive teacher education for special educational needs and disabilities: some more thoughts on the way forward. *Teaching and Teacher Education, 61*: 164–78.

Schoonover, N. R. (2021). Exploring visual literacy skills and dispositions through a museum-sponsored online professional development for K-12 teachers. *Journal of Visual Literacy, 40*(1), 71–89.

Shaw, A. (2017) Inclusion: the role of special and mainstream schools. *British Journal of Special Education, 44*(3): 292–312.

Sigurjónsdóttir, H. B. (2015) Cultural representation of disability in children's literature. In Traustadóttir, R., Ytterhus, B., Egilson, S. T. and Berg, B. (eds), *Childhood and Disability in the Nordic Countries: Being, Becoming, Belonging*. London: Palgrave Macmillan, pp. 115–30.

Thomson, R. G. (2017) *Extraordinary Bodies: Figuring Physical Disability in American Culture and Literature*. New York: Columbia University Press.

CHAPTER 5

DfE (2010) *Equality Act*. Available at: https://assets.publishing.service.gov.uk/media/5a7e3237ed915d74e33f0ac9/Equality_Act_Advice_Final.pdf. Accessed 28 August 2024.

DfE (2014) *The Young Person's Guide to the Children and Families Act 2014*. Available at: https://assets.publishing.service.gov.uk/media/5a7dc4b0e5274a5eb14e7114/Young_Person_s_Guide_to_the_Children_and_Families_Act.pdf. Accessed 28 August 2024.

DfE and Department of Health (DoH) (2015) *Special Educational Needs and Disability Code of Practice: 0 to 25 years. Statutory guidance for organisations which work with and support children and young people who have special educational needs or disabilities*. Available

References

at: https://assets.publishing.service.gov.uk/media/5a7dcb85ed915d2ac884d995/SEND_
Code_of_Practice_January_2015.pdf. Accessed 28 August 2024.

gov.uk (2022) *SEN Review: Right Support, Right Place, Right Time*. Available at: www.gov.uk/
government/publications/send-and-ap-green-paper-responding-to-the-consultation/sum-
mary-of-the-send-review-right-support-right-place-right-time#:~:text=The%20SEND%20
review%20sets%20out,healthy%20and%20productive%20adult%20lives. Accessed 28 August
2024.

gov.uk (2024) *Special Educational Needs in England. Academic year 2023/24*. Available at: https://
explore-education-statistics.service.gov.uk/find-statistics/special-educational-needs-in-
england#releaseHeadlines-summary. Accessed 28 August 2024.

Hartley, R. (2010) Teacher expertise for special educational needs: filling the gaps. *Policy
Exchange*. Available at: www.policyexchange.org.uk/wp-content/uploads/2016/09/teacher-
expertise-for-SEN-jul-10.pdf. Accessed 28 August 2024.

HM Government (2023) *Special Educational Needs and Disabilities (SEN) and Alternative Provision
(AP) Improvement Plan. Right Support, Right Place, Right Time*. Available at: https://assets.
publishing.service.gov.uk/media/63ff39d28fa8f527fb67cb06/SEN_and_alternative_provi-
sion_improvement_plan.pdf. Accessed 28 August 2024.

Koster, M., Pijil, S. J., Nakken, H. and Van Houten, E. (2010) Social participation of students
with special needs in regular primary education in the Netherlands. *International Journal of
Disability, Development and Education*, 57(1): 59–75.

Pearson (2024) *School Report 2024: Your Voices, Our Future*. Available at: www.pearson.com/
content/dam/global-store/en-gb/schools/insights-and-events/topics/school-report/2024/
School-Report-2024-WEB.pdf. Accessed 28 August 2024.

UNESCO (2009) *Policy Guidelines on Inclusion in Education*. Available at: https://unesdoc.
unesco.org/ark:/48223/pf0000177849. Accessed 28 August 2024.

CHAPTER 6

Bizumic, B., Mavor, K. I. and Platow, M. (2017) *Self and Social Identity in Educational Contexts*.
London: Routledge. https://doi.org/10.4324/9781315746913

Brown, C., Douthwaite, A., Donnelly, M. and Olaniyan, Y. (2024) *Belonging, Identity and Safety
in London Schools*. Research and policy briefing on behalf of London's Violence Reduction
Unit. Available at: www.london.gov.uk/sites/default/files/2024-01/Belonging%2C%20
identity%20and%20safety%20in%20London%20schools%20UoB%20for%20
VRU%284%29.pdf. Accessed 28 August 2024.

DfE (2014) *The National Curriculum: Key Stage 1 and 2*. Available at: www.gov.uk/national-
curriculum/key-stage-1-and-2. Accessed 28 August 2024.

DfE (2021) *Guidance: Personal, Social, Health and Economic (PSHE) Education*. Available at: www.
gov.uk/government/publications/personal-social-health-and-economic-education-pshe/
personal-social-health-and-economic-pshe-education. Accessed 28 August 2024.

Dixon, L. and Hales, A. (2014) *Bringing History Alive through Local People and Places: A Guide
for Primary School Teachers*. London: Routledge. https://doi.org/10.4324/9780203111963

gov.uk (2024) *Schools, Pupils and Their Characteristics: Academic Year 2023/24*. Available at: https://explore-education-statistics.service.gov.uk/find-statistics/school-pupils-and-their-characteristics#. Accessed 28 August 2024.

Hess, D. J., Lanig, H. and Vaughan, W. (2007) Educating for equity and social justice: a conceptual model for cultural engagement. *Multicultural Perspectives*, 9(1): 32–9. https://doi.org/10.1080/15210960701334037

Hjörne, E., van der Aalsvoort, G. and de Abreu, G. (2012) *Learning, Social Interaction and Diversity: Exploring Identities in School Practices*. Rotterdam: Sense. https://doi.org/10.1007/978-94-6091-803-2

Kelley, N. and De Santos, R. (2022) Attraction, identity and connection in Great Britain in 2022. *Rainbow Britain*. Available at: www.Stonewall.org.uk. Accessed 28 August 2024.

Mandela, N. (1990) *Nelson Mandela visits Madison Park HS in Roxbury in 1990*. Roxbury, MA: GBH News.

Refugee Council (2024) Available at: www.refugeecouncil.org.uk/. Accessed 28 August 2024.

Sanders, J. and Munford, R. (2016) Fostering a sense of belonging at school: five orientations to practise that assist vulnerable youth to create a positive student identity. *School Psychology International*, 37(2): 155–71. https://doi.org/10.1177/0143034315614688

Tajfel, H. (1979) Individuals and groups in social psychology. *British Journal of Social and Clinical Psychology*, 18(2): 183–90. https://doi.org/10.1111/j.2044-8260.1979.tb00324.x

Thapa, A., Cohen, J., Guffey, S. and Higgins-D'Alessandro, A. (2013) A review of school climate research. *Review of Educational Research*, 83(3): 357–85. https://doi.org/10.3102/0034654313483907

Tosh, J. (2015) *The Pursuit of History: Aims, Methods and New Directions in the Study of History* (6th edition). London: Routledge.

CHAPTER 7

Allarakha, S. (2024) What are the 72 other genders? Gender identity list and child awareness. *MedicineNet*. Available at: www.medicinenet.com/what_are_the_72_other_genders/article.htm. Accessed 28 August 2024.

Barnes, E. and Carlile, A. (2018) *How to Transform Your School into an LGBT+ Friendly Place: A Practical Guide for Nursery, Primary and Secondary Teachers*. London: Jessica Kingsley.

DfE (2010) *Equality Act*. Available at: https://assets.publishing.service.gov.uk/media/5a7e3237ed915d74e33f0ac9/Equality_Act_Advice_Final.pdf. Accessed 28 August 2024.

DfE (2011) *Teachers' Standards: Guidance for School Leaders, School Staff and Governing Bodies*. Available at: https://assets.publishing.service.gov.uk/government/uploads/system/uploads/attachment_data/file/1040274/Teachers__Standards_Dec_2021.pdf. Accessed 20 March 2022.

DfE (2013) *The National Curriculum in England*. Available at: https://assets.publishing.service.gov.uk/government/uploads/system/uploads/attachment_data/file/425601/PRIMARY_national_curriculum.pdf. Accessed 20 March 2022.

References

DfE (2020) *Relationship Education, Relationships and Sec Education (RSE) and Health Education: Statutory Guidance for Governing Bodies Proprietors, Head Teachers, Principals, Senior Leadership Teams and Teachers*. Available at: https://assets.publishing.service.gov.uk/media/62cea352e90e071e789ea9bf/Relationships_Education_RSE_and_Health_Education.pdf. Accessed 28 August 2024.

Fearon, J. D. (1999) *What is identity (as we now use the word)?* Unpublished manuscript. Stanford University, CA.

gov.uk (2024a) *Government to Lay New Law to Halt the March of Gender-neutral Toilets in Buildings*. Available at: www.gov.uk/government/news/government-to-lay-new-law-to-halt-the-march-of-gender-neutral-toilets-in-buildings. Accessed 28 August 2024.

gov.uk (2024b) *Schools, Pupils and Their Characteristics: Academic Year 2023/24*. Available at: https://explore-education-statistics.service.gov.uk/find-statistics/school-pupils-and-their-characteristics#. Accessed 28 August 2024.

Page, M. L. (2017) From awareness to action: teacher attitude and implementation of LGBT-inclusive curriculum in the English language arts classroom. *Sage Open*, *7*(4): 1. https://doi.org/10.1177/2158244017739949

Rasul, Z. (2022) Game over for discrimination and sexism in women's football. *Stop Hate UK*. Available at: www.stophateuk.org/2022/07/19/game-over-for-discrimination-and-sexism-in-womens-football/. Accessed 28 August 2024.

Silveira, J. M. and Goff, S. C. (2016) Music teachers' attitudes toward transgender students and supportive school practices. *Journal of Research in Music Education*, *64*(2): 138–58.

Splitter, L. J. (2007) Do the groups to which I belong make me? Reflections on community and identity. *Theory and Research in Education*, *5*(3): 261–80. https://doi.org/10.1177/1477878507081790

CHAPTER 8

Clair, J. A., Humberd, B. K., Caruso, H. M. and Roberts, L. M. (2012) Marginal memberships: psychological effects of identity ambiguity on professionals who are demographically different from the majority. *Organizational Psychology Review*, *2*(1): 71–93. https://doi.org/10.1177/2041386611429041

DfE (2011) *Teachers' Standards: Guidance for School Leaders, School Staff, and Governing Bodies*. Available at: https://assets.publishing.service.gov.uk/government/uploads/system/uploads/attachment_data/file/1040274/Teachers__Standards_Dec_2021.pdf. Accessed 28 August 2024.

DfE (2013) *Geography Programmes of Study: Key Stages 1 and 2. National Curriculum in England*. Available at: https://assets.publishing.service.gov.uk/government/uploads/system/uploads/attachment_data/file/239044/PRIMARY_national_curriculum_-_Geography.pdf. Accessed 28 August 2024.

Department for Education and Skills (DfES) (2005) *Developing the Global Dimension in the School Curriculum*. Available at: https://dera.ioe.ac.uk/6152/7/globald_Redacted.pdf. Accessed 28 August 2024.

Disney, A. (2005) Children's images of a distant locality. *International Research in Geographical and Environmental Education*, *14*(4): 330–5.

Houghton, S. A., Yumiko, F., Lebedko, M. and Li, S. (2013) *Critical Cultural Awareness: Managing Stereotypes Through Intercultural (Language) Education*. Newcastle: Cambridge Scholars.

Maude, K. (2023) EAL and SEND: the same but different? In Conteh, J. (ed.), *The EAL Teaching Book* (4th edition). London: Sage.

Milner, C. (2020) Classroom strategies for tackling the whiteness of geography. *Teaching Geography*, *45*(3): 105–7.

Moghaddam, F. M. (2002) *The Individual and Society: A Cultural Integration*. New York: Worth.

National Geographic (2022) *Encyclopaedic entry: place*. Available at: https://education.nationalgeographic.org/resource/place. Accessed 11 September 2024.

Noxolo, P. (2017) Introduction: decolonising geographical knowledge in a colonised and re-colonising postcolonial world. *Area*, *49*(3): 317–19.

Ofsted (2011) *Geography: Learning to Make a World of Difference*. Available at: https://assets.publishing.service.gov.uk/government/uploads/system/uploads/attachment_data/file/413723/Geography_-_learning_to_make_a_world_of_difference.pdf. Accessed 28 August 2024.

Ofsted (2021) *Research Review Series: Geography*. Available at: www.gov.uk/government/publications/research-review-series-geography/research-review-series-geography. Accessed 28 August 2024.

Picton, O. J. (2008) Teaching and learning about distant places: conceptualising diversity. *International Research in Geographical and Environmental Education*, *17*(3): 227–49.

Refugee Council (2024) Available at: www.refugeecouncil.org.uk/information/refugee-asylum-facts/separated-children-facts/. Accessed 28 August 2024.

Said, E. (1978) *Orientalism*. New York: Pantheon.

Save the Children (2018) *Hear It from the Teachers: Getting Refugee Children Back into Learning*. Available at: www.savethechildren.net/sites/default/files/Hear%20it%20from%20the%20Teachers.pdf. Accessed 28 August 2024.

INDEX

ability and disability, 100–101
ableism and neuronormativity
  challenging, xiv, 65–82
  in classroom (case study), 70–71
  defined, 65
  inclusive educational practices in, 74–76
  inclusive strategies to support children with SEN, 76–80
  issues arising from inclusion and labelling, 76
  see also special educational needs (SEN)
academic and social outcomes, enhancing, xii–xiii
academic support, 132
Accelerated Reader, 44
access to opportunities, ix
accountability, and transparency, x
achievement gaps, reducing, 141
advocacy, 58
age, 101
agencies, collaboration with, 132
Agenda for Sustainable Development (2030), 108
agender, 103
Ainscow, M., 51
Anti-Bullying Alliance (ABA), 14–15, 94
Anti-Bullying Week, 94
Anti-Racism Initial Teacher Training (ITT) Framework, 2
anti-racist, 2
  application in, x–xi
  globalisation and, 121
  promoting equity in, 141
Arizona State University, 38
asylum seekers, 91, 101, 119, 128
attainment
  at Early Years and Key Stage 1, 21
  socio-economic status and, 19–20, 23
attainment gap, 20–21, 25, 44
attention-deficit/hyperactivity disorder (ADHD), 56–57
autism spectrum disorder (ASD), 56

BAME, 2
Barnes, E., 107
BBC Teach website, 96–97
Beckett, A., 59
belonging
  and inclusion in schools (case study), 88
  and respect, x
Better Health Channel, 54
Black History Month, 93–94
Black Lives Matter movement, 4
Blakeman, E., 50
Booth, T., 51
Boyd, A., 65, 83, 98
boys' attainment (case study), 46
Brexit referendum (2016), 3
British Red Cross website, 90
Browne, K., 42
bullying
  peer-on-peer, 7
  preventing and tackling, 3

  racial, 6
  racist, 3

Çalışır, G., 36
canalisation, 38
career aspirations, 42–43
careers, 47
Carlile, A., 107
cerebral palsy, 54
Cheyne, R., 58
Child Poverty Action Group website, 28, 33
children
  access to high-quality teaching, 78
  with ADHD, 56–57
  attending school, 25
  in care, 102
  and communal identity, 84
  developing cognitive abilities, 40
  and disability, 51–55, 61–62
  Early Learning Goals, 21
  from economically disadvantaged backgrounds, 21–23, 25, 27
  educational outcomes of, 6
  eligible for FSMs, 20–21, 24
  ensuring equal opportunities for, 3
  ethnic minority backgrounds, 6, 8, 94
  experiences of schools, variation in (case study), 24
  free education for, 23
  LGBTQ+ awareness, 93, 108
  marginalised, 116
  poverty impact on, 20
  preparing, for diverse world, 141
  refugee and asylum seeker, 128, 132–136
    case study, 130–131
  requiring SEN support, 69
  resources needed for, 87
  responsibility for SEN children, 72–74
  with SEN, 57, 75–80
  sense of belonging, 87
  teaching about refugees, 90
Children and Families Act (2014), 73
chronic health conditions, 54
citizenship and nationality, 101
City of Sanctuary UK, 91–92
Clark, C., 44
classes, and socio-economic status, 19–20
classroom diversity, addressing, 140
Classroom Secrets, 60
classroom visuals, 116
colour blind, 6
communal identity, xiv–xv, 83–97
  cultural engagement, 87–88, 91–95
  defined, 83
  facets of identity, 86
  formation of, 84–85
  inclusion and belonging, in London schools (case study), 88

in-group and out-group separation, 85–86
school identities, 86–87
subject inclusion, 89–91
Cook, A., 61
Cook, M.C., 47
cost-of-living crisis, 26–27
Covid-19 pandemic, impact on academic progress, 25–28
critical cultural awareness, 120, 125–126
critical thinking and empathy, xii
cued speech, 55
cultural calendars, 9, 127
cultural competence, ix, 109, 136, 140
cultural elements, teaching, 89
cultural engagement, 83, 84, 87–88
promoting, in school, 91–95
cultural sensitivity, 132
curriculum
bias, 9
constructing culturally diverse, 116
English national, 121
on geography, 90
history, 89
including globalisation into, 121
inclusive, x
lack of representation in, 8
non-racist, 7–8
Currie, D. H., 41

Davies, L., 1, 18, 119
Davis, J. M., 52
deafness and silence (case study), 55
delegated budget, 77
De Menezez, J.C., 4
dependency culture, 125
deprivations, 5, 129
reducing, 19
disability(ies)
ability and, 100–101
defined, 50
exclusion, 51–52
reducing, 60–61
mental, 56–57
physical, 54–56
SEN and, 57, 67–68
disability visibility
in literature, 58–59
in teaching resources, 60
discrimination, xv, 76, 93, 107
disparities, in educational attainment, 53
disruptive behaviours, 75
distant places, 120, 121–124
effective teaching of, 126–127
diversity, ix
diversity, equity and inclusion (DEI), in teaching, ix, 140
Dixon, L., 89
Down syndrome, 76
Dräger, J., 25
dual coding, 132

early career teacher (ECT) experience, 122
Early Years Foundation Stage framework, 21
economic injustice, xiii
attainment, at Early Years, 21
attainment gap, 20–21, 25
Covid-19 pandemic, impact on academic progress, 25–28
government initiatives, 29–30
historical socio-economic inequalities, 23

leadership and governance, 29
physiological and safety risks for poverty at home, 23–25
poverty-proofing, 29
primary/secondary schools, 22
role of ITT providers, 31–32
scale of the problem, 20
socio-economic status and attainment, 19–20
education
Education Act (1944), 23
educational foundation, 140
educational outcomes
gender differences in, 41–44
gender roles and behaviours on, 39–40
education health care plans (EHCPs), 51, 69
Elementary Education Act (1891), 23
11-plus test, 23
empathy, fostering, xii
End Violence Against Women, 4
engagement and participation, x
English as an additional language (EAL), 120
environmental deprivation, xv, 129
Epstein, D., 41
equality, xvi
Equality Act (2010), 3, 19, 29, 35, 51, 53, 66, 67, 99, 107, 116
Equal Pay Act (1970), 42
equitable assessment, in classrooms, x
equity, ix–x
in education, xi, 141
ethnicity, 101–102
defined, 1
race and, 2
ethnic minority, in schools
representation, 8, 102
subcultures, 9–10
ethnocentrism, 9
exclusion, through disability, xiv, 50–64
children living with disabilities, in UK, 53
children with SEN, 57
deafness and silence (case study), 55
evidence of good practice, 62–63
mental disabilities, 56–57
physical disabilities, 54–56
reasons for, 52
reducing disability exclusion, 60–61
shift towards inclusive education, 53–54
teacher experiences working with disabled children, 61–62
visibility, 57–60
Extraordinary Bodies (Thomson), 52

fairness
and justice, ix
promoting, xi
family, and identity, 102
feminism, impact on society, 42
Floyd, G., 4
free education, 21, 23
free school meals (FSMs), 18, 20, 21

Gay Rights movement, 93
Gender Action Portal, 47
gender and sexuality, celebrating in foundation subjects, 109–115
gender attainment gap, 45
gender bias

157

Index

careers, 47
  impact on higher education, 47
  importance of reducing, 46–47
gender boundaries in play (feminist movements), 38
gender, defined, 35, 102
gender differences, in educational outcomes, 41–44
  career aspirations, 42–43
  factors affecting gender divides, 41
  feminism, impact on society, 42
  reading for pleasure, 44
  school sport gender restrictions (case study), 43
  school subcultures, 41
  societal changes, 42
  sport and extra-curricular activities, 43–44
  teacher influences, 41–42
gender discrimination and sexism
  boys' attainment (case study), 46
  gender differences in educational outcomes, 41–44
  gender roles and behaviours on educational
     outcomes, 39–40
  gender stereotypes, 38–39
  girls, in STEM subjects, 45–46
  importance of reducing gender bias, 46–47
  reducing gender differences in schools, 47–48
  role of gender during primary socialisation, 36–37
  schools in reducing gender stereotypes, 40
  school sport gender restrictions (case study), 43
  in schools, xiii–xiv, 35–49
gender divide, 35, 41
gendered behaviours, 36
gender equality, 108
  promoting through picture books
     (case study), 108
genderfluid, 103
gender-neutral toilets, 103
gender reassignment, 102–103
gender segregation, 44
gender stereotypes, 38–39, 40, 44, 47, 108
Gender Trust, 42
geography
  discipline of, 122, 123
  effective teaching of distant places in, 126
  and identity formation, 90–91
  lesson planning, 122
  as medium for exposing 'explanatory relationships', 121
  national curriculum, 124
  stereotypes in, 124
  teacher subject knowledge, 124
Gillborn, D., 6
Girls' Career Aspirations (Ofsted), 42
girls, in STEM subjects, 45–46
global competence, 141
globalisation
  defined, 120
  and education, 121
  and environmental deprivation, xv, 119–139
  impact, on UK, 120–121
Goff, S. C., 109
Gorard, S., 20, 23
Gurian, M., 35

Hales, A., 89
hate crimes, 4–5, 107
hierarchy of needs, Maslow's, 24–25
high-quality teaching, accessing, 78
historical socio-economic inequalities, 23
history, in identity formation, 89

hobbies, 103
Holiday and Food programme (HAF), 28, 33
homosexuality, 107
Houtte, M. V., 41

identity, xv, 84, 99–100
  ability and disability, 100–101
  age, 101
  aspects of, 100–107
  citizenship and nationality, 101
  ethnicity, 101–102
  facets of, 86
  family, 102
  gender reassignment, 102–103
  hobbies, 103
  languages spoken, 103–104
  personality, 104
  personal, xv, 98, 100
  physical appearance, 104
  political views, 104
  profession, 105
  race, 105
  religion, 105
  sex, 105–106
  sexual orientation, 106–107
  social class, 106
  values and beliefs, 106
illiteracy rates, 20
imaginative geography, 124
immigration and colonialism, 4
impairments *see* disability(ies)
inclusion, x, xvi
  and belonging, in London schools (case study), 88
  in education, 74
Inclusive Britain report, 2
inclusive classrooms, fostering, 141
inclusive classroom strategy checklist, 136–137
inclusive communities in classrooms, fostering, 127–128
inclusive curriculum, x
inclusive education, 11, 53–54, 75
inclusive educational practices
  in challenging ableism and neuronormativity, 74–76
inclusive school culture, 60
inclusive strategies, to support children with SEN, 76–80
  access to high-quality teaching, 78
  creating positive learning environment, 77
  evaluating teaching, 78
  intervention access, 79
  teaching about SEN, 79–80
  understand pupils and their needs, 77–78
  work effectively with TAs, 79
inclusive teaching strategies, 60
independent schools, 26
Index of Multiple Deprivation, 5
individualised support, x
individualised teaching, 141
inequalities, in educational outcomes, 23
in-groups, 83, 85–86
intergroup bias, 85–86
intersectionality, x
ITT Core Content Framework, 32

Jackson, C., 41

Kearney, A., 51
Keil, S., 57
Key Stage 2 Attainment, 41

158

language, 103–104, 116
  barriers, 128, 132
  support, 132
leadership and governance, 29
learning disabilities, 57
Legender, R., 119
legislation, policies and, 3
LEGO, 42–43
LGBTQ+ communities, 93, 107, 109
LGBTQ+ Equality Action Plan, 108
liberal chauvinists, 6
literature, disability representation in, 58
Long, R., 53
looked-after children, 102

Mandela, N., 92
marginalised, xvi
  identities, 100, 107–108
Martinez, T., 39
Maslow's hierarchy of needs, 24–25
Maude, K., 119, 140
McRobbie, A., 42
Mead, M., 36–37
mental disabilities, 56–57
Mentally Healthy School website, 96
Mitsos, E., 42
mobility impairments, 54
multilingualism, 136

Narsaria, A., 39
National Centre for Computing Education, 45
National Education Union (NEU), 15
nationality and citizenship, 101
National Literacy Trust website, 92
needs, Maslow's hierarchy of, 24–25
neuronormativity
  defined, 65
  promoting, 66–67
  see also ableism and neuronormativity
Newcastle University, 29
New York University, 38
non-racist curriculum, creating, 7–8
non-racist person, 2
Not only Pink and Blue website, 39, 49

Oakley, A., 37, 38
Ofsted, 3, 42, 121, 124
Ogden, J., 61
out-groups, 83, 85–86
overt racists, 6

parental approach, to different gender roles, 37
parental attitudes toward gender-neutral toys, 39
parental engagement, 132
peer-on-peer bullying, 7
personal identity, xv, 100
  defined, 98
  wheel, 118
personality, 104
personal, social, health and economic education
    (PSHE), 90
  PSHE Association, 117
physical appearance, 104
physical disabilities, 54–56
physiological and safety risks, for poverty at
    home, 23–25
place attachment, 90

place identity, 90
policies and legislation, 3
political views, 104
Pope, C., 40
poverty
  impact on children, 20
  physiological and safety risks for, 23–25
  race and, 5
Poverty-Proofing the School Day initiatives, 29, 30–31
Pride Month, 93, 116
primary schools, 22
professional development, 140
profession/occupation, 105
Programme for International Student Assessment
    (PISA), 19, 23
Public Sector Equality Duty, 3
Pupil Premium (PP), 18, 29–30

qualified teacher status (QTS), 31–32
quality first teaching (QFT) approach, 133

race, 105
  defined, 1
  and ethnicity, 2
  and poverty, 5
racial bias, in schools, 6
racial bullying, 6
racial injustices, 4
racial stereotypes, 3
racism
  addressing, in primary schools, xiii
  curriculum bias, 9
  effective practices, 10–11
    case study, 12–13
  ethnic minority representation in schools, 8
  ethnic minority subcultures in schools, 9–10
  teacher racial bias, 6–8
  in UK schools, 6
  understanding, 2
  unintentional racism in schools, 9
racist bullying, 3
reading for pleasure, 44
recognition of differences, ix
refugee children (case study), 130–131
refugee pupils
  challenges faced by, 128–129
  teachers supporting, 132–137
refugees/immigrants, 90, 101, 119, 128
Refugee Week, 92, 116
religion, 105
religious education (RE), 89–90
representation of diverse groups, ix
Robinson, D., 62
Roper, K., 98

safe and supportive environments, x
Said, E., 124
Sapouna, M., 7
SATS tests, 22
school climate, 87
schools
  communal identity, 84–87
  cultural engagement in, 88
  equity and diversity in, 88
  ethnic minority representation in, 8, 102
  ethnic minority subcultures in, 9–10
  funding, 27

159

Index

gender discrimination and sexism in, xiii–xiv, 35–49
primary/secondary, 22
promoting cultural engagement in, 91–95
promoting neuronormativity in, 67
reducing gender differences, 47–48
reducing gender stereotypes, 40
resources in, 87, 92
of sanctuary, 91–92, 130–131
SEN in, 67, 68–70
shift towards inclusive education, 53–54
sports (case study), 43
subcultures, 41
unintentional racism in, 9
secondary schools, 22
self-fulfilling prophecy, 6
sensory impairments, 54
sex, 105–106®
defined, 35
Sex Discrimination Act (1975), 35, 107
sexual orientation, 106–107
Sharpe, S., 42
Shaw, A., 54
Siddiqui, N., 20, 23
Sigurjónsdóttir, H. B., 59
Silveira, J. M., 109
social class, 19, 106
social cohesion, 53, 89, 121
social-emotional skills, building, 141
social identity, 83
Tajfel's theory of, 85
social inclusion, 21, 31, 92
social justice
advocating for, 141
promoting, xii
Social Mobility Commission, 19
social mobility, disparities in, 19
societal diversity, xi–xii
socio-cultural theory (SCT), 100
socio-economic disparities, 3, 4, 8
socio-economic status (SES), 18
and attainment, 19–20, 23
special educational needs (SEN), 53
and Alternative Provision Green Paper, 72, 74
Code of Practice, 67, 68, 73
disability and, 57, 67–68
education health care plans and, 69
identified conditions leading to SEN support, 69–70
inclusive strategies to support children with, 76–80
label, 76
plans, 69
responsibility for SEN children, 72–74
in schools, 67, 68–70
teaching about, 79–80
special educational needs and disabilities (SEND), 66
Special Educational Needs and Disability Code of Practice: 0 to 25 Years document, 73
special educational needs coordinator (SENCO), 62, 69, 77
sport and extra-curricular activities, 43–44
STEM subjects, 45–46
stereotypes
formation of, 124–125
media influence, 125
Stevens, K., 35

stigma, 76
Stimulating Physics Network, 45
structural racism, 5
subcultures, 9–10, 41, 46
subject inclusion, 89–91
geography, 90–91
history, 89
personal, social, health and economic education (PSHE), 90
religious education (RE), 89–90
subjective social status, 20
Sustainable Development Goals (SDGs), 108
Sutton Trust, 21, 34
systematic synthetic phonics (SSP), 55
systemic inequities, addressing, xii

Tajfel's theory of social identity, 85
talk partners, 78
teacher experiences working with disabled children, 61–62
teacher racial bias, 6–8
teachers, exemplar medium-term plan 1for, 109–115
Teachers' Standards, 125
teaching assistants (TAs), 27, 63, 79
teaching resources, disability visibility in, 60
toy stereotypes, 38–39
transparency, x
trauma-informed practices, 132
tripartite system, 23
Trussell Trust, 20
Twinkl, 60, 93, 95

unconscious racial bias, among teachers, 7
Uncu, G., 36
unintentional racism, in schools, 9
United Nations Convention on the Rights of Persons with Disabilities (UNCRPD), 53
University of Plymouth, 47
US Bureau of Labour statistics, 47

values and beliefs, 87, 106
Veness, G., 1, 35, 50
violent/unsafe behaviours, 75
visibility, 57–60

Wallace, J.B., 42
Watson, N., 52
withdrawn behaviours, 75
women
academic performance, 47
discrimination against, 107
hate crime prevalence for, 107
sexual assault, 4
Women in Science Day website, 45
World Day for Cultural Diversity for Dialogue and Development, 92–93
world-mindedness, 126
world religious festivals, 94–95

xenophobia, 3

YouGov, 38

zones of regulation, 77